AF263638

THE ARTICULATED MAN

First published 2014 by James Zul
The Articulated Man
© 2014, James Zul

All rights reserved. This book contains material protected
under International and Federal Copyright Laws and Treaties.
Any unauthorised reprint or use of this material is prohibited.
No part of this book may be reproduced or transmitted in
any form or by any means, electronic or mechanical, including
photocopying, recording, or by any information storage and
retrieval system without express written permission from the
author / publisher

A CIP catalogue record for this book is available from the
British Library

Articulation = a) A jointing together or being jointed together;
b) The method or manner of jointing.
Man = Mankind.

ISBN 978-0-9929797-0-6
Ebook Mobi 978-0-9929797-1-3
Ebook Epub 978-0-9929797-2-0

Cover image courtesy of NASA
Cover design by Joe Russ

The veil is lifted on the intersecting realities that surround us all, and the hidden meanings of the synchronous experience explored within the context of one person's life.

CONTENTS

THE ARTICULATED MAN

A Personal Journey Through the Universe of Consciousness

JAMES ZUL

DID YOU FALL OR WERE YOU PUSHED?

I took my young daughter to the swing park the other day. We were joined by a grandmother and her three granddaughters–ranging from about three to eight years. They all wore matching summer dresses and plimsoles, as if they had come from a birthday party or christening. In a warm but posh manner, the dialogue went something like this: "Ok, girls, come along. Let's play on the climbing frame first. Careful now, one at time. Mandy help your sister; careful now, don't want to get hurt. Now, up we go, Susan, Rachel… mind your step; hands first, then follow with the legs. Easy does it. Now, girls, let's do the slide. Over we go… You first, Mandy; you're the youngest. Must be cautious here. Now, you next, Susan; Rachel, you behind. Watch she doesn't fall. Right, down we go, jolly good… Over to the swings next."

"Grandma Curtis, can I go on the roundabout? I'll be careful."

"Mmm. Well, just you then, Rachel–as you're the oldest. Daddy will be along soon."

"Can I go on the swing, Granny?"

"Okay, then, Mandy. Let's take it slowly, though. Do as I say and you won't get hurt."

"Grandma, push me on the roundabout…"

Grandma Curtis sounded like a nice sort; eager to entertain the girls and concerned for their wellbeing. But, if I was a social psychologist or management consultant, I would be in no doubt that she was micro-managing their every move and instilling fear at every juncture.

This type of exchange was all too familiar during my childhood. It had a deflating effect on family outings and from an early age sowed the seeds of suspicion that parents weren't as perfect as you would have liked to believe. I would be well into my teens before being able to articulate to myself the underlying mechanisms at work.

Though, I can't say I wasn't warned. After all, my parents bought us books of fairy tales–from *Hansel and Gretel* to *Rapunzel*–and took us to the cinema to see perennial classics such as *Snow White* and *The Wizard of Oz*. Explicit and compelling characterisations of the "rapacious" mother figure or the conniving witch were at the forefront of these plots.

Shortly after my daughter was born, I visited her in the maternity ward, which housed five other mothers and their babies. The father of a beautiful little girl was in attendance in the next cubicle, with his mother-in-law at the bedside. The room must have been about 35 degrees celsius and he was mopping the sweat from his brow. His daughter was lying in a cot next to her mother's bed and was wrapped in a woollen suit and hat and covered with a blanket. He instinctively began to fan the baby and removed the knitted hood and pulled down the blanket. The grandmother immediately replaced them, even though she was only garbed in short-sleeves and light trousers. Did she feel uniquely placed to decide what was suitable treatment for the baby based on her gender or past experience with children, or was it a blind concern that was oblivious to the discomfort that might be imposed on the baby? Who was being cruel and who was being kind, I wondered.

Few would argue that gender roles have been demarcated to facilitate work and family obligations, but also to cement power structures. Human civilisations have in the past given prevalence to the feminine attributes, as it were. Think of the Oracles at Delphi and other ancient societies where the intuitive powers of women were highly regarded. Perhaps that is why later communities switched to a patriarchal system, in an attempt by "man-kind" to reclaim some power. As Lady Elizabeth, in *The Other Boleyn Girl*, says to her daughter: "Observe the ladies of the court. See how they achieve what they want from their men, not by stamping their little feet, but by allowing the men to believe that they indeed are in charge. That is the art of being a woman." By the time of Henry VIII, it would be no surprise if such an attitude had gained credence among elements of England's female populace.

To return to fairy tales, the woodcutter was alert to the threat from the marauding wolf, but he missed the presence of the witch.

But let me offer another perspective on these distinctions of male and female; one that traverses the realms of the esoteric experience–for that, might I suggest, is where other, more dynamic archetypes reside.

When I think back on my childhood, the overall impression is one of frustration and embattlement. Nonetheless, I had another life; one that was lucid and abides to this day. It took place at night. Dreams are not the only playground of the mind. The personality complex I know as myself has inhabited dimensions, or etheric zones, that are more clear, dynamic, interactive, psychic and embracing than the one I find myself while writing these words. The "education" offered by the schools I attended by day was insignificant, and indeed rendered ridiculous by the encounters and visions afforded me by night. Interactions with entities both sublime and grotesque gradually instilled a sense of self-worth and inner confidence. It is not easy to convey the multifaceted nature of that expanded state in mere words. But let me try, for you too may have accessed it.

By the age of 14 I had an assuredness about my place in the nocturnal aether. Sometimes I would find myself watching a film of myself walking down the street; only the visual emphasis would be on the "energetic" interaction between myself and other people. On other occasions I would encounter beings of such majesty that my template, and aspirations, for human potential would be forever altered.

One such encounter was with a female consciousness that was immediately overwhelming in her countenance. You might say she utterly outclassed me. Only abstractions can hint at her perfection and maturity, for there is no linguistic scale I know of that can capture her essence adequately. She possessed a passive power that could absorb any activity I might throw at her; a limitless womb–dark and infinite. To feel her gaze was to know complete acceptance; a nurturing and fertile ground for the "self". This was the ultimate stasis, where the thrashing, juvenile nature of the male–my male–disposition was inconsequential in its effect, and yet I was perceived by "her" with total benevolence. To behold this "mother" figure was to be totally overawed, and perhaps that was the lesson for me that night; to place me in a wider context.

There is a Hindu prayer–the Devi Kavacha (the Armour of Divine Mother)–which says, *ajita vama parhsve tu dakshine ca aparajita*: "O Divine Mother, be on my left as Ajita (invincible) and on my right as Aparajita (the One who is never defeated)." I wonder if people know what power they summon by uttering these words with sincerity.

Some seven years later, while lying on my bed and feeling waves of despair wash over me, I passed out. Perhaps it was a nervous breakdown; it was certainly a relinquishment of control and of identity–a dissolution of the self.

Almost immediately I found myself in a black void; but surrounded by a dozen "light beings". I gazed into the "body" of the one in front of me and immediately felt its complete understanding of every facet of my life, and also a recognition of a greater, fuller self that had been around for a lot longer. Its body–comprised of light but in a human shape–seemed to contain a whole universe of wisdom and experience. Indeed, I could feel the regard of each of them upon me, like a long lost family reunited after eons of time. Their joy at our reunion was child-like; unencumbered by restraint and pure of intention. "Oh, let me stay here with you forever," I thought to myself. "This is all I could ever desire". Then we were flying; with them ranged out on either side of me, escorting me through the void.

The next thing, I turn around to face a huge, amorphous ball of light. At that moment I became subsumed within this great consciousness; and yet still identifiable as "myself"–the meagre personality. A voice said: "It does not matter what you do or do not do in your life," and then hinted, as it was a mere gentle suggestion, that I would return hence to this state. And what a state; the woven, intricate omniverse stretched out to the ends of creation; whole galaxies seemed like small enclaves of activity, and all of it contained within a structure that was overwhelming in its perfection. The apparent random disorder, the machinations of free will everywhere were still configured to have "perfect' outcomes. The physical sensation, if there was one, was of being stretched, in an energetic sense–as if I had reached out to grasp a football pitch, and somehow managed to contain it within my arms. And yet this great mind was me, and I was it. A father beholding its favoured son, and the son incredulous at forgetting this great Truth; as it was indeed a remembering of sorts. The exquisite wisdom and compassion (how inadequate those words are) of my escorts were apparent here again but taken to an unfathomable scale–the ultimate intimacy between Father and son and simultaneously the great inheritance revealed. If only this configuration of letters could encrypt something of that essence.

When I came round the next morning, my existence seemed to have been re-set; the months of depression were but a distant memory; emblazoned on the inside of my eyelids were the words: "Everything is all right".

After that experience, the terminology of the biblical began to make more sense. To commune with the "Father" is to inherit the kingdom; to gaze out on all of creation and behold its utter perfection–as an extension of the self; subsumed within the great light; the overarching consciousness.

Father	Mother
The "Light"	The "Dark"
All is revealed	Beguiling enigma
Outward expansion	Inner universe

Neither of these aspects–the perfected Father and Mother–offer any imposition on the separate beholding personality, and yet reveal themselves with total selflessness.

To be held in their embrace is to know complete security; the freedom from the deluded machinations of self-will; the fear of mortality.

Just as the shaman or adept will be put through terrifying ordeals and physical agonies in pursuit of a pure mind, so it seemed my experience over two decades had been contrived (by something larger than myself) to bring me to a "breaking point". A mind that is constantly challenged and indeed perplexed by its surroundings is one that is awake, at least–and the trivial blandishments make way for a crystallisation of focus and consciousness. To put it another way: slowly, consistently, methodically the ego was paired back–expunged–until a clear void loomed ahead–with an unobstructed view (and path) back to Source. The trick is to hold that vision after being resubmerged into the melee of noise and confusion in the sensory world.

Such a journey should not be confused with a masochistic pursuit of "pain", rather the pattern of its higher machinations were at one level apparent, if perplexing and unpleasant to the ego mind. Indeed, what might amount to adversity for one person would be a walk in the park for another.

Some years later, at a workshop on meditation, I encountered a being, or at least its consciousness, that exemplified and "embodied" the attribute of gratitude–to such an extent that it infused me with bliss. My intuition was that this consciousness had reached a state of oneness with "God" and, on realising the regard it was held in by the Father\Mother, actually became that state of gratitude–that archetypal vibration. After all, to know it is to become it. And by gratitude, I mean also the attendant realisation of total security and humility– provided by that motherly and fatherly embrace.

Gratitude; Humility; Security

HOME AND AWAY

My biological father instilled in me a desire to "succeed" in the world; to become a top advertising man, or a great newspaper editor. My father had become a respected journalist, after spending a childhood in considerable poverty and suffering a harsh domestic environment. He left school at 15 and yet was well read and a brilliant chess player—once challenging the Russian champion Anatoly Karpov to a game. Though he embraced intellectual pursuits and increased the material comforts of life, he remained acutely aware of the hypocrisies inherent in his leafy suburban landscape. His interlocutions to get on in life, I think, were both a call to remain safe from the constraints of poverty and also to rise above the social pretence of the burgeoning "middle classes". He no doubt imagined that to surmount a corporation or community was to escape its grip.

The mould was thus set. While the other children exchanged football stickers and posters of Ford Cortinas, I daydreamed of owning a beautiful mansion, of driving Aston Martins, and of building a corporate empire that would somehow emancipate, rather than enslave, its employees.

The creative and dynamic possibilities of the media–first advertising, then public relations and laterally newspapers–drew me in. My focus was laser-like, and few could resist my introductory letters. Once I was in the door, the person who had hired me could expect nothing less than total dedication and the pursuit of perfection. Of course, it soon became apparent that I was something of an anomaly; my colleagues had other priorities–whether it be their families or what they were going to watch on TV that night, their energies were dispersed more widely or more carefully contained. Having such a voracious animal in their midst must have irked some, but for the company boss I was always a gift.

In a blaze of activity, time passes quickly, and it was not long before "promotions" were being thrown my way. However by then the novelty of submitting completely to corporate objectives had worn off, and indeed I had scarcely any more energy to give to a more demanding job. For me, the company had become the father and mother figure that I otherwise lacked; its security blanket was a costly trade-off–identification in exchange for my free thought, free action and free time.

Ultimately–though there are blessings inherent in any social interaction and disciplined effort–this material focus is to worship a false god. Selfless devotion and generosity of effort are all too commonly absorbed by less conscientious colleagues and later by the top executives or shareholders milking the profit margins. As is happening at an alarming rate–with profit margins and executive bonuses spiralling while economies of scale shrink on the "shop floor"–these corporate entities become conduits for the slavery of a consumption-led society.

HARD OR SOFT?

Leaving behind the social charms of Winnipeg, my family returned to Glasgow in 1980. This provided a searing initiation into the hard routine of street life–that is to say wondering the streets unsupervised as a youngster. It is not something you see much of these days–children seem much more subject to the determinism of the media (which proclaims that the outside world is inherently dangerous) and technology (which also conveys that perception of danger, albeit in the form of a more interactive narrative). Regardless of what I might describe in the following paragraphs, I still don't believe in danger–at least not as a haphazard, chance event.

While on a visit to my paternal grandmother, who lived in one of the city's outlying housing estates, I noticed a bin lorry parked outside–seemingly abandoned at the side of the road. As I peered into the vacuous container at the rear, a small, timid dog looked back in terror, perhaps aware of his imminent fate at the hands of the metal crusher. He may have been a stray raking about for food or maybe he had been literally thrown out by his owners.

On another occasion, on entering a bedroom at the back of the flat, a squint-eyed boy appeared at the gaping window, even though it was seven feet above ground level. No doubt he was desperate to take ownership of the toy that had been left on the window sill. My youngest brother–no more than a toddler–was left momentarily in the front garden one day–just as a local youth was passing by. The young thug took the opportunity to jump the fence and kick my brother in the head, then casually leaped back onto the street and went on his way. Many years later, I came across a newspaper interview with a former gangster who had grown up on that street. He seemed to believe that it had produced a succession of violent criminals. Though he didn't mention the statistics on missing dogs.

My maternal grandfather had a farmstead in southern Ireland. When a chicken was required for dinner, he would come out to the yard and select the nearest hen, and simply wring its neck. While visiting on holiday as a ten-year-old, I came across an old snare in the barn and dutifully set it to prone. Sometime later, on being alerted by squeals, I discovered a black rat caught by its tail in the trap. Living up to my manly expectations, as I saw it, I battered the poor brute to death with a stick–rather than just release the coil. Insensitivity was the order of the day, and I had just passed muster[1].

Without an alternative role model or paradigm, the consciousness can also become trapped–into thinking a hard shell and brute force are the only ways to navigate

---

1 As I ponder again this folly of my youth, a warm, benevolent presence begins to envelope me; a wordless voice from the past–that has never really gone away–who fills the space in the absence of noise and a chattering mind. A reassuring embrace that translates into words as: "It was done in innocence; a firm belief in the validity of the action, much as instinct compelled that rat and others to take live prey for sustenance." And so says the Father.

a harsh world. Human nature's response to danger has been expressed as a fight or flight–to respectively adopt an identity as a tough guy or to reconcile strategies of avoidance. However, there are those people who remain impervious to the apparent antagonisms of such ghettos by maintaining a focus on themselves; they don't take any external events personally, and take an imaginative leap elsewhere. And where the heart yearns, the legs soon follow.

More recently, while at the swing park with my young daughter, the man beside us let his daughter climb up onto the swing unaided. When she got her leg stuck in the chain and began panicking, he kept his distance. When I instinctively moved to catch her, he raised his hand to dissuade me. That young girl was not going to be mollycoddled, even if she broke her neck in the process.

Much has been written about the prevalent patriarchal values of society, not least by articulate feminists. In the world of commerce, the women I have encountered who set out to climb the ladder, while professing feminist ideals, seem merely to be imitating their ambitious male colleagues. They often embody the self-centred, careerist drive but without the humour or collegiate sensibilities of their male counterparts. The effect on male colleagues under them can be of emasculation, and the women of alienation. They may be heading in the direction of the boardroom, but also a looming black hole of consciousness.

History books are full of acts of cruelty inflicted by male-dominated institutions and states; think of the Spanish Inquisition; the Conquistadors' treatment of the native South Americans; not to mention the Portuguese and Dutch colonialists; the Roman church's pursuit of Cathars and Templars, to name but a few; the English Crown in its quest for a commonwealth. Indeed, it seems the public schools in England are still trying to turn out independent-mined, ruthless colonialists–only they end up running corporations these days instead of foreign "jurisdictions". Then there were the regimes of Adolf Hitler, Joseph Stalin, Benito Mussolini, Francisco Franco, Mao Zedong. It is no longer a great secret that many of these men and their acolytes were in fact insecure, embittered and physically weak. And yet they were focused. Large parts of their respective societies courted them and bought into their warped visions, but also helped produce their psychopathy in the first place.

This active, masculine impulse has shaped the foundations of western civilisation. No wonder some women feel obliged to play men at their own game. But what of the others?

Latin and Celtic nations in particular put a value on machismo and "strength" in their men. Many mothers demand it of their sons. A "strong" man is desirable, the perceived wisdom goes, and many women buy into the dream. They may discover down the line that the word "strong" should have been substituted for "unbalanced" or "catatonic". They may resent the societal deceit imposed on them and resort to subterfuge.

Of course, there is nothing really to stop anyone taking stock of their life and challenging the norms and expectations directed at them from schools, family members and the work place. And yet many people would rather follow the guidance of some authority figure–be it the media, government, health board or pub gossip–even on the most erroneous rationale. The Wizard of Oz has never been so busy.

Popular culture celebrates the narcissist–the predatory male. Think of James Bond (though that is not to write off the Bond character entirely) and every rock star that ever pulled on a pair of leather trousers. Ah, someone with self-confidence, we say, they must know something we don't. Writers and programmers are careful to sculpt such characters and present them in dynamic situations that they ultimately traverse. The rest of us watch them and spend our time trying to emulate their ease of passage through life, but in doing so often overlook the effects we have on all the other players in our personal stories. If the other person's perspective was at the forefront our minds the way our goals or desires were, then the story might have a much better ending. And the path we tread through life might have less of that often unseen debris.

REVENGE IS BITTER-SWEET

"Suffer little children, and forbid them not, to come unto me: for of such is the kingdom of heaven." Luke 18:16.

Modern narrative is less candid about the narcissistic female.

To use an analogy from the natural world, some women are honey bees and others are wasps–but the wasps usually think they are honey bees, and their offspring are only too happy to believe it–at first. The children grow up thinking they have been nurtured by a honey bee and employee a cognitive dissonance to reconcile their frequent and lasting psychological "stings". Until they realise that they grew up in a wasp's nest, they will not understand the hidden, pervasive influence of their mother–or the acquiescence of their father.

While queueing for a cinema ticket recently, I noticed that the place was mainly filled with twenty and thirty-something couples. The man in front of me was enthusiastically explaining his plans for the week ahead to his girlfriend. Her response was muted, in fact she continued to cast around the room, seemingly more interested in the decor. In frustration, he exclaimed: "You never listen to me."

"Yes I do," she replied glibly, looking down at the floor.

More on that later, but consider the undermining effect on a dependent child of such brusque dismissals.

Much light has been shone into the psychological ramifications for children of alcoholic parents. The father or mother, or both, in their self-indulgent addiction to drugs or drink focus the attention of the family on their needs. Without the binding cohesion of love and consideration, an emotional vacuum descends on the household. The day-to-day maintenance of the children's needs get sidelined; the emotional and practical support they require as they go through school can be absent; if the father is dependent on alcohol, for example, his partner may feel unloved and instead develop strategies to elicit "energetic sustenance" from her children. This can take the form of criticism–every decision or comment they utter is slapped down. It can be plain old neglect–the subconscious subtext of which for the child is, you are not worth even bothering about. Some children, forced to seek refuge from one parent's chaotic behaviour will invest their emotions in the other. If the other parent has developed an unhealthy control drama with their offspring, then they become even more subsumed by it. The mother, or father, may blame the children for binding them to family obligations and a relationship that otherwise would have ended. Again the children become subjected to both verbal and non-verbal statements that they are worthless or troublesome.

But alcohol, or any other addiction, is a mere manifestation of the self-obsessed personality.

More often than not, it's what's implied, rather than spelt out, that registers most deeply.

The tendency among adult humans to assume that they always know what's best for younger members of their species takes on new dimensions when contained within the bounds of the family unit. I once sat next to a mother and her teenage son at a cafe. They had ordered tea and cake; the son took a bite of his cake and grimaced. He called over the waitress to complain; when he began to explain to the waitress what was wrong, his mother burst out laughing. On the rare occasions when my father would engage in conversation, he would often cut you off just as soon as you began to speak, so in effect he would conduct the conversation himself–asking the questions and then answering them. At the dinner table as children, if we uttered a word, he would tell us to "shoosh", so as not to interrupt whatever programme was on TV. We were once left in the car for an evening while he and my mother went to dinner at an Indian restaurant. Nobody begrudged them the culinary respite, but the symbolic effect endures to this day.

Disempowerment leads to frustration, which leads to resentment–be that women in a patriarchal society; children in a dysfunctional family or men or women in unbalanced relationships.

The ultimate revenge is when the parent–embodying the corrupted form of the feminine or masculine template–"ruins" the children. The female is most often placed by convention to affect these outcomes, while the man blithely pursues his obsessions in work, sport or social life.

Of course, the assassination of the self experienced by some children at times allows for a more considered reconstruction of identity later in life, with the attendant attributes of empathy and open mindedness. This may be one factor in the universal appeal of the rags to riches narrative in popular fiction–from *The Ugly Duckling* to *Alibaba*. To quote Christopher Booker[2] on the process of self-realisation: "It was in them all along; they have matured; realised their potential."

To use storytelling parlance, what is the arc of this theme? The confused, out-of-place youth has undergone a process of transformation. Their resplendent, glowing countenance or new-found status are merely reflections of inner clarity–the attainment of their highest potential.

The energetic exchange underlying social interactions–or I should say "control dramas"–has been documented in books such as *The Celestine Prophecy*[3] and *The RA Material*[4]. For example, the "Intimidator", the "Interrogator", the "Aloof" person and the "Poor Me" types. Those of an orthodox scientific or conventional psychological stance may find such concepts unpalatable. But there can be no doubt that we exist in an energetic reality–vibrating particles, made up of protons, neutrons, quarks and so on.

A much-overlooked consideration of science is the fact that the observer of an experiment can and often does influence the outcome. Experiments by the Princeton Engineering Anomalies Research unit suggest that human consciousness can affect the outcome of seemingly "random" procedures; ordinary participants are able to affect computerised random number generators and change the speed with which radiation emanates

2 Booker, Christopher, The Seven Basic Plots, Continuum, 2004, Page 51

3 Redfield, James, The Celestine Prophecy, Warner Books, 1993

4 McCarty, James Allen; Elkins, Don; Rueckert, Carla, The Ra Material: An Ancient Astronaut Speaks, Whitford Press, 1984

from a source as measured by a Geiger counter. Cleve Backster[5], a former interrogation specialist with the CIA, used polygraph experiments with plants to demonstrate that hateful thoughts will destroy them, while directed feelings of love will enhance them. Jagdish Chandra Bose, the Indian scientist, proposed that plants had a sensitive nervous system and responded to shock by a spasm just as an animal's muscle does. He went as far as administering poisons and fire to metals such tin, zinc and platinum and plotted their fatigue responses on a graph–experiments that demonstrated a cyclical fatigue response in both stimulated cells and metals, as well as a distinctive cyclical fatigue and recovery response across multiple types of stimuli in both living cells and metals.

Just because so-called inanimate objects or simple organisms are not readily engaged through our five senses does not mean they are without feelings or awareness at another level. Therefore it would seem that consciousness, or conscious intent, has an affect on that which we would perceive as matter.

A camera merely provides a snapshot of the photographer's consciousness at that moment–that is why a photo speaks a thousand words; if you were able to look back down the viewfinder, you would no doubt glimpse the internal workings of the shooter's mind.

"God created mothers because He cannot be everywhere to serve His creation."

Inscription on a church yard wall, India.

---

5 Jensen, D., The Plants Respond: An Interview with Cleve Backster, 2006

"Because I'm worth it."

L'Oréal advertising mantra.

Arguably–and there is considerable scope for debate–men have less to unravel than women, as they have been subject to a societal construct that was mostly of their own making. Their ego-derived sense of self and self-worth are necessarily more explicit in the day-to-day dance of social interaction. For those of the determinist view that men and women are simply wired differently, so are directed by genetic impulses, I would point to the body of work on environmental effects on behaviour to balance that perspective. Indeed, if our corporate and government benefactors really thought that DNA dictated the ebb and flow of life, why would they put such effort and resources into telling us what to think, eat, consume. On a more subtle and sinister level, the saturation of the media with celebrity on one hand and war/criminality/terrorism on the other suggests an understanding of the pervasive and destructive effect of judgmentalism and fear on populations. Given the consolidation and tightly controlled ownership structures in place, there is not much escape from this homogenous discourse, unless you seek out alternative voices through the internet or community groups–or switch off your TV and radio altogether.

Without a comprehensive awareness of Self[6],a person is susceptible to such forces. Look at the radical shift in behaviour among soldiers in battle zones; the group dynamics of crowds at a concert; of football fans during disruptions at matches, even of some shoppers at the January sales. Heaven help the child who consistently

---

6 Self, with a capital S, denoting the higher faculties or Soul.

challenges the received wisdom of his school's agenda or the military recruit who questions his orders. The arbiters of punishment for transgressing the status quo are in the first example his or her classmates and in the latter the other recruits. The system, as it were, polices itself. Why? Because no doubt it is unsettling for many people to have their unquestioned assumptions about their place in society challenged.

People react with surprise when they hear news that an organisation or government has committed this or that transgression against the public–for example, pharmaceutical groups falsifying clinical data to get their drugs approved, or a food conglomerate poising the water supply to save money on disposal costs. Even a cursory glance at the component parts of those groups–i.e. its workers–will reveal its collective state of mind, and possible behavioural consequences. If we are employed by an organisation, we buy into its vision or direction, to a lesser or greater degree. Some people don't like the culture of the place and will leave soon afterwards, others will draw a veil of ignorance and go along with the programme, others will actively identify with the leaders and aspire to their position or values. I once worked for a large media group which had a high-profile and right-wing chairman. It would not be an exaggeration to say that the hierarchy from managing directors, editors, assistant editors to journalists was a ripple down effect of that potent archetypal figure at the top. That company has both an explicit "news" agenda and what could be described as an "emerging" agenda (also covering what will not be included in the "news"). What seemed interesting to observe was that the lieutenants did not need explicit instructions from their leader; they already embodied his values and perspective, and so were already propagating his world view and objectives.

It is not that dissimilar in our relationships with the external organisations we engage with–there is some implied trust, or else why would we be tuning in?

At times of disenchantment or fatigue brought on by the hypocrisies and impositions of this rather contrived societal structure, it can be useful to seek out a "reset". One that has appeared to me at times of stress–where my sleep has been affected–is the pure, sweet aroma of the early morning air. It can be intimidating to encounter its unfamiliar yet profound presence as it suddenly enters the nostrils and pervades the lungs–like brushing against a beautiful woman on the early morning train, when sleep and wakefulness have not yet been fully demarcated, and we are unsure as to which realm the experience belongs.

THE PECKING ORDERS

I would like to introduce you to "Anna"; at face value, she is a real person; she can talk, think and move. But if you were to peer into her mind, you would find a personality complex that is not anchored to anything more substantive than the body's chemical and biological relay system. At an early stage in her life–perhaps after some trauma–her etheric cords[7] were severed, and some time later she made the decision to attach them to another person–possibly the same person behind her original trauma. Here are some clues to who that person might be. While growing up, her father was absent, both emotionally and in person. Her mother was domineering and opinionated, but at least she was there to offer guidance–albeit with a certain vitriol. Her own views, ideas, decisions will have been criticised and undermined by her wilful mother, so that her emotional development was stunted early on and her sense of identity tied to the mother's whims. Any desire or conviction of thought would be offered up for mother's approval, and if it fell short, or was deemed too dangerous or ridiculous, then she would dismiss it as another flawed creation of her inadequate self. In adolescence and into adulthood, she will have been attracted to men who seemed confident and dynamic. With recurring certainly, she would find

---

7 A psycho-spiritual attachment, or "lifeline".

those men to be vexatious and narcissistic–ultimately unreliable and unfaithful. After a succession of such engagements she will have done some "soul searching" and surmised that integrity would perhaps be more easily found in the more reserved, humble type of man.

Her period of self-reflection will have been so brief and superficial that any of the fundamental questions about her own psychological make-up and underlying motives will have remained unanswered.

Now she will turn her attention to the less domineering sub-species; while simmering with frustration and anger at what she has previously suffered at the hands of "men".

The new, modest model of man is at first a welcome relief from the tardy and untrustworthy predecessors. However, it is not long before she is missing the strong opinions and domineering nature of the narcissist. She begins to fantasise about characters on TV–archetypal figures who will once again sweep her off her feet and release her from the responsibility of making her own decisions or being alone with her own nature.

Doubts will begin to creep in about the value of her new partner–who turns up when he says he will and takes his share of domestic duties–because after all, deep down, who of value could be so committed and respectful to someone as unworthy as her, she asks herself.

Gradually her mood becomes more cantankerous as the facade of the gentleman crumbles under the weight of her underlying beliefs about "men". The more the man displays concern for her deteriorating mood, the more irritated she becomes with his "pandering" behaviour.

And so, once again, the unrealised template or perception asserts itself. He feels an emotional gulf; nothing to bind them; no real commitment or common ground. Indeed, in public she often seems embarrassed about his presence. What he doesn't see are the invisible cords binding her to her mother, and perhaps even her mother's mother, as the net of control stretches back through the generations.

The empathetic man–and a child may be on the scene by this stage–begins to wonder about her sanity and plots his exit. When he finally packs his bags, she sinks back into the swamp of victimhood and further asserts her disdain for mankind, faced with this new batch of supporting empirical data.

If they do stay together, she will continue to project her feelings of inadequacy onto him and will devote her energies to psychological attacks–through goading comments or even hysterical outbursts–justified by the underlying image she has fabricated through her selective interpretation of her experiences. Never will she brave the depths of her own psyche and instead will wear the mantle of victimhood, vacillating between a "poor me" and "interrogator" stance. Eventually the hen-pecked man–and potentially any children–will either become withdrawn and uncommunicative or he will rebel with violence–something formally alien to his character. To her, his attentive, nurturing tendencies were formally evidence of weakness, and now aggression emerges as proof of his inherent brutality.

And can they expect a balanced understanding from social services or the police, should it escalate into family breakdown or accusations of assault? Yes, and no.

Because domestic strife is so prevalent in crime statistics–including murders and myriad forms of physical abuse–the government takes a pragmatic stance, politically at least. If a woman makes a complaint of assault against a man, generally, he can expect to be arrested by the police without question. This mechanism serves a purpose, of course–to distance the people involved and provide the deterrent to further aggressive behaviour–whether that be a stern warning or more extensive prosecution.

However, it is not without its flaws. A senior detective confided in me that there were many men who "get put away for nothing". While men are simple to deal with, women can be an unknown quantity, he said. "They can lie, exaggerate, twist, and the blame will remain with the man." He maintained, however, that it was considered political dynamite to highlight these apparent injustices. These, one hopes, are exceptions to the otherwise solid rule. I make the point, not to excuse any form of brutality, but to highlight the destructive effects of self-delusion and manipulation. Whereas the emotionally-fuelled outburst can wreak havoc as it travels outward, equally the emotional chasm of victimhood can suck the unwary into its void–the sympathetic partner, the social worker, the neighbour, or whole sections of society. Indeed, the modern industrial-medical-chemical system fosters and is sustained by such a mindset, not to mention the media.

LEAN, MEAN AND GREEN

"Ask, and it shall be given you; seek, and ye shall find; knock, and it shall be opened unto you." Matthew 7:7-11

How refreshing and uplifting is the aroma from the newly pruned garden; the birds trumpeting their appreciation of the largesse of worms and bugs, and mother nature enlivening our senses with her delicate perfume. What perceptual revival awaits those who trim back the overgrowth of the ego mind? What fertile ground lies beneath the layers of habitual behaviour?

The disappointments in the people around me began mounting up at an early age. It would often be with incredulity that I observed the common penchant for selfishness and ignorance among both both young and old. Pettiness seemed to be the default setting for humanity. Then, aged about eight, I was taken on holiday to Ireland.

One day, while lost amid the fields and woodland of county Cork, my consciousness began to open—at least it perceived a whisper from the land; a wordless utterance that said, "I am alive."

Standing, staring into a crop of trees and bushes, I felt a thousand eyes peering back out at me. I could feel their attention; their pondering of my awareness. "How much does he know about himself," they wondered. "Do we know him better than he knows himself?"

There was no judgment, just being was enough. To perceive their subtle energies was the only key to entry; to be initiated into the realm of Nature, without cost or expectation–a wholly inclusive club.

"We remain hidden, but present," they suggested, "until the time you are ready to wake up more fully, and view things the way they really are. In the meantime," they whispered, "forget us not; go forth and tell our story, should you wish. Enchant others the way we enchanted you with this glimpse."

Thus was revealed yet another template for life; something pure and unadulterated. Existence for its own sake was enough reason for being.

Perhaps, I wondered, this explained the homely, ingratiating behaviour of the locals. Had their proximity to this invisible mind of Nature had set the benchmark?

The sense of vulnerability induced by being lost in an "alien" landscape must have opened a chink in the armour of the ego, allowing in the rays of an uncommon spectrum. Concurrently the conventional perspective of the little self was temporarily shunted aside, allowing the bigger Self to peer out through those eyes and discern with those ears.

To sit atop a tree in this rural idyll was to feel the warming embrace of motherly hands, permanently outstretched, entreating the heavens. Perched on the middle branches of a large cedar or oak, the world down below seemed needlessly preoccupied; a fox foraging below or a grazing cow would never know the peace and comfort afforded by my green-fingered host.

That consciousness–call it Mother Earth–would seek me out once more, and to do so she would co-opt whatever outlet she could find; in this case, an electronic box situated in my living room. Her siren call came one Saturday afternoon as I was alone flicking through the television channels–all four of them. This time I heard her voice clearly with my ears, it was no higher perception, though she misconstrued my name–"Raaaaaaw-bin… The Hooded Man…" What an exquisite, transcendental revelation to behold the voice of Nature manifest in human form–in the guise of a noble musical venture known as Clannad. TV had finally grown up: the subtlest and most endearing harmonic subtext imaginable to flank an elegant and poignant telling of the Robin Hood story (*Robin of Sherwood* was produced by HTV and Goldcrest for Britain's ITV station). Saturday afternoons would henceforth be sacred–at least for the two-year run of the series.

Many years later, after graduating from university, I would return to Ireland to work. My arrival coincided with the onset of the Celtic Tiger boom, where the country's economic expansion outpaced its European counterparts. The once austere urban landscape began to buzz with the excitement of new-found wealth. American corporations led the inward investment but also helped to import the values of capitalism; get it while the going's good, was the mantra. It seemed to me that much of the old decency and generosity had been washed away as the population chased the deluge of cash. New cars rolled out of the showrooms and housing estates sprang up faster than fields of clover.

Anyone taking a taxi or buying a house at that time would have come face to face with the "unacceptable face of capitalism", to quote a former British prime minister. The "cute hoor" tactics perhaps cultivated during the British occupation were now directed at anyone–particularly with a foreign accent–carrying a wallet. To engage with a cab driver was to meet with brazen attempts at extortion; to make an offer on a house was at times a slow waltz with a phantom bidder–on an already sky-high price tag.

The media proclaimed the blandishments on offer and the formally humble felt lifted to greatness–if only they could get their hands on some of that largesse.

The government even introduced a special incentive savings scheme, with very generous terms of interest, to reduce the amount of money in circulation. Now, a decade or more on, as the country reels from a banking crisis and property bubble, with many more people mired in debt, tied to negative equity on their homes and with far fewer jobs on offer, the boom-time dream must seem like a hoax to many people. Instead of every man for himself, could not the country's leaders have developed a sovereign wealth fund (to be deployed with the benefit of hindsight) and invested in the infrastructure of schools and hospitals. Indeed, why did they not go further and take the opportunity to reconfigure the status quo; to re-examine the old structures developed under British dominion, and embrace more egalitarian, humanistic models of society?

Going back to the Middle Ages, the English intellectual class–the ecclesiastic orders–viewed Ireland as a pastoral society lacking in order and barbarian in its simplicity. It was the mindset that would justify intervention in some shape or form, and was given added credence when Pope Adrian IV (an Englishman) issued his papal bull, the *Laudabiliter*, in 1155 giving Henry II the right to assume control over Ireland and impose some homogeneity on the disparate abbey system. The problem with the monasteries was that each had the autonomy to develop and extend its own interpretations of the gospels according to common sense, rather than blind dogma. Indeed, those scattered churches that took an interest in the more esoteric facets of the scriptures would have been even more divergent from Rome's party line.

Ireland's geographical location–stuck on the edge of Europe–had distanced it from interfering hands and allowed it to maintain its Gaelic agrarian society (cultivation of family ties and the land, albeit with inter-clan rivalries) long after many landlocked nations had been brought under the fold of feudalism. The *Laudabiliter* paved the way for the first Norman invasion, that would soon follow–and the battle to subvert the Gaelic/pagan mindset raged for hundreds of years hence. The trumpeted Celtic Tiger boom in the noughties, to me, seemed like the masterstroke that finished off the last vestiges of Ireland's pastoral dream. Just as Ireland had carefully packaged and exported its "Emerald Isle" image to the world–in the form of material goods and tourism–so now it would be subject to the propaganda of the industrial edifice it had courted. The compelling and dynamic "image" of material wealth had finally dissolved the fading picture of the humble pagan ideal. Or did it?

The country may have been denuded of its once famous forests, but this is not to say that the surface cannot be repopulated and re-beautified under the stewardship of each family willing to create their own oasis. A pragmatic and organic Emerald Isle can rise from the ashes of its chemical and mechanical desolation–but on an individual basis, where each person has the opportunity to cultivate their own space for food and sustenance; a place where trees, shrubs, flowers, vegetables and fruit exist in symbiosis and provide the vital Earthly link that humans so desire. The cord may have been cut, but it can be re-grown with determination and patience. Let the policymakers start distributing plots to families in perpetuity–free of tax binds–and watch the wonder and magic of Ériu[8] once more unfold.

America had its Great Depression in the late 1920s and into the 1930s. Some people say it was prompted by the Wall Street crash of 1929, others that the stock market crash was a symptom of the economic slump. Either way its effects were pervasive and long-lasting. Some years ago Gershwin's "Rhapsody in Blue" came on the radio as I was mulling about in the kitchen. Its signature melody emerged as a siren call; almost immediately images from a bygone era began to form in my mind; the unique architectural landscape of New York became apparent; one person's mind became open to me, then another and another, until the collective mindset of that time was revealed. It felt like the 1920s and it was clear that despair had taken hold; the daily grind of labour and the diminished dreams of economic salvation were pulling these people into a void of hopelessness. But behold, as this ethereal tune swept over the city, I felt the

---

8 The modern Irish Éire evolved from the Old Irish word Ériu, which was the name of a Gaelic goddess.

delight and fascination in the minds of the masses as a new paradigm registered in their consciousness–the collective consciousness. This was no political soundbite or government handout, but a harmony from heaven proclaiming that all was well. If a human could compose such a dynamic, ingenious melody, what couldn't he do, they thought. As the full movement played out, it seemed like each distinct section took the listener through a new stage of upliftment and renewal–the heavy fog of despair dispersed by the power of harmonics.

My father was an ardent fan of the Russian composers Dmitri Shostakovich[9] and Sergei Prokofiev, and so whenever there was an orchestra in town reciting their works, we–as a family–would be there, usually in the front row. It is one thing to be in the presence of live music, particularly of the classical variety, but the weight of consciousness conveyed by the music of these brilliant, haunted men is enough to dispel notions of time and space. Even with my age still in single digits and with no knowledge of their personal histories, their trials and vicissitudes–and those of the Russian people–would unfold before me in the concert hall. The harmonic spectrum went beyond words, and carried the emotion and pathos, and terror, of Stalin's regime into the present–to be accessed by any who dared tune in. Not only that, but the minds of these two composers–or at least their signatures–remained, as an explanation of their underlying motives and experience. So powerful was their focus–not doubt the result of extreme oppression–that their music became the encoded experience, almost as real as the lived life. To those in the audience willing to temporarily let go of themselves, the full immersive encounter awaited. Perhaps that was my father's secret

---

9 See Appendix: Short Fiction–Some Minor Revisions

garden–where, having disabused himself of any notions of intellectual snobbery and remained a humble progeny of the Gorbals, was able to enter that other world in the utmost privacy of a hall containing several thousand spectators. That is the great service of such musicians–to allow others to benefit from their experience without having to go through the full "ordeal" as a life lived.

As the Rune stones would say, consider the uses of adversity.

The 1990s were a decade of cultural exuberance for Ireland. This was perhaps best exemplified during the interval act of the 1994 Eurovision Song Contest, which the country was hosting for the second year running. Who could have imagined what was about to leap off the stage as the audience quieted for the start of the interval act. "Riverdance" was a seven-minute, three-part suite composed by Bill Whelan, featuring the Celtic choral group Anúna and choreography by Michael Flatley. For me, sitting in my living room, this exquisite journey into traditional melody and dance was nothing less than the land itself speaking. It had an instant familiarity, and yet engaged the senses in a way that promised deliverance from a humdrum existence. Not unlike the band Clannad some years before, the spirit of nature had conspired to reveal herself through these disparate artists; and not any old spirit, but one particular to Ireland–motherly, enchanting and dynamic. "Here I am," she said, "unsullied by the modern world and able to engage you as I did of old."

While researching a film script set in the 12th century–often referred to as the "Dark Ages"–I tuned into someone living among a community during that time. Looking around at the people in his vicinity, this individual exalted in the beauty and purity of his companions. Their attire was crisp, clean and simple and their consciousness was attuned to their benevolent surroundings–a green, hospitable landscape. These people existed at a more instinctual level–at one with their surroundings, and their environment was in turn tuned to them–ready to dispense its largesses in a prescribed and anticipatory manner. The technocratic society lauds its superiority over Nature. Man–or at least a certain type of person–has sought to master and tame the natural world, which they regard as hostile, overwhelming in its complexity and unpredictable. But these are the people who have remained in their primordial selves–their reptilian centres–whatever you want to call it. However, when you begin to open your consciousness to other sensory perceptions outside the five basic ones, the natural world becomes something entirely cognizant, mostly benevolent, and an "intelligence" that can be one of your greatest allies. Instead of trying to decimate a system of breathtaking elegance through destruction of eco-systems, industrial pollution, and so on, man is uniquely positioned to engage with and co-create with this collective mind. What were the sages of old doing in their caves? Why did they choose the wilderness over a metropolis to seek enlightenment? They were learning to let go of their basic faculties so that they might open themselves to many others–on another spectrum of awareness. To observe the tight co-operation of bees or ants or flocking birds is to witness the outward workings of their over-arching mind, one not tied to an individual brain, but expansive in its perspective while being intimately connected to each member of that species.

Even if you can escape to a place free of traffic, overhead aeroplanes, pylons or any other human activity, it is not silence that you discover, but a harmonic rhythm–crickets chirping, the exclamations of birds, the wind whispering through the trees. What soothing tones compared with the jarring buzz of modern appliances: computer hard drives, WiFi devices, fluorescent lights, and even, at a more subtle level, the electricity grids criss-crossing the land. Many would say the dull headache they get from watching television is a small price to pay for the information and entertainment that it provides. I would suggest that there are greater insights and delights to be discerned from a communion with Nature.

As I write this, London hosts it Open Garden Weekend, where the public is given access to private gardens around the city, from Georgian town houses to the courtyards within housing estates and even private barge gardens on the Thames. Normally hidden away, these oasis of natural beauty draw together their communities in a focused effort to maintain and enjoy their verdant bounty. Here too mother nature reaches out and nurtures bonds between people.

Today's stream of popular culture–whether it be pop music, TV drama or feature films–lacks any such magical quality. Indeed, one wonders if any heed is paid to subtext in the stories that now get told. As a handful of corporations have taken hold of the means of production and its distribution channels, the currency of creativity has become devalued. This may be the product of bean counters calling the shots or it may be more contrived; a purposeful dumbing down of society.

To ask, "what are they leaving out" can be more revealing than to consider what they are putting out. But I leave that up to you.

THEIR BARK IS WORSE THAN THEIR BITE

Some years ago I stumbled upon a kennel on an industrial estate. In actual fact, I had accepted a lift from someone who stopped off there on some business–not entirely above board, I suspect. I got out of the car and followed him in to the corrugated building, just to stretch my legs, but was met by a large and aggressive Rottweiler–luckily it was in a fenced enclosure. On spotting me, it launched into a frenzy of barking and clawing at the mesh; it clearly had only one thing on its mind. Then, from the enclosure next to it, an even more rabid creature sparked up–in the form of a muscle-bound pit bull, which directed its blistering anger at the Rottweiler. To this day, I don't know what these dogs had been bred for or what had been done to make them so psychotic, but the level of aggression on display was almost enough to break through the metal barriers that separated us. There would be little anyone could do out in the open against such ferocious intent. To the other two men present, this was a pleasing spectacle. No doubt, in the world they inhabited, the display of power, or force, was something to be proud of. Of course, people can also slide down the scale into their more animalistic instincts–having been brutalised and undermined from an early age. If the dogs, or the people, were able to gaze beyond the red mist of hate, they might once again glimpse the more subtle instruction and benevolence emanating from the subtle realms–where a greater part of themselves resides. Often the first step is to see through the motives and mechanisms of their tormentors, and then move on from a more placid standpoint to gaining a larger perspective, i.e. accepting that there must have been causes in this life or other lives that brought about those experiences. Sometimes, as children, we pick up the psychological cues from our parents about how to view the world and how to behave in various circumstances. If we go through life with unquestioned obedience to our parents, then we will perhaps follow them blindly down the same dark alleyways. If your intention–taking the larger perspective–was to be born into a dysfunctional family in order to break the cycle, as it were, then at some point you will need to take a step back and look for the patterns. Dogs might not be able to readily do this, but they can be offered a fresh paradigm–of gentleness and respect–and reformulate their conditioned responses too. Most living beings crave acknowledgment–and every single one of them deserves it. In its absence, the rot sets in…

On a cycling trip some years ago, we stopped at a rural pub for lunch. My three companions and I were the only customers, save a man sitting on his own in the corner of the room. He looked typically rugged, in an agricultural sort of way, though there was something that distinguished him that at first eluded me. I'm not in the habit of staring at people, but needed to satisfy my curiosity. On further inspection, it became clear that he was wearing a toupee–and it was back to front. When his food arrived, he immediately coveted it by bending a protective arm around the plate. He must have noticed my interest because he bared his teeth at me, much like a dog guards a trophy meal. Perhaps he had spent his entire life among animals–who also had little sense of fashion–but had enough pride to seek out an ill-fitting wig. It was a Friday–perhaps pay day–and the chance to splash out on some well prepared fodder, rather than fighting for scraps out in the "wilderness".

On several occasions I have come across people who were there but who were not there–in other words, ghosts. And they pop up when you are least expecting it. I once got dragged along to an air show with some friends. Although it was out in the agricultural belt the security procedure at the entrance was quite elaborate, and therefore was the last place you would expect to meet a "tramp". I was standing looking at some stationary aircraft, perhaps fairly vacantly, but was aware enough to know that I was not in proximity to anyone else; or was I? As I turned around for the second time in about a minute, a large, scruffy, dishevelled man stood beside me. His black beard was matted and his face bore the mottled brown patches of someone who hadn't washed in a very long time. Even more worrying was the white puss running down his nose. However, his attention was not on me but on the space just ahead of us. He looked lost, or in some kind of trance. I turned away to gather my thoughts, then swivelled back to say something–but he was gone. And he didn't duck into some side street or behind a tree; there were only miles of open fields.

Charles Dickens created vivid and compelling characters that live on well after you have read his books. His stories were astute social critics and the racial memory of those squalid times remains in the architecture and "social space" of London. Greenwich is one such place and it bridges many of Britain's epochs, given its role as an important maritime centre. I had the pleasure of living there for some years, in close proximity to the maritime college. One frosty morning, as I shuffled along the river bank to catch a ferry to London Bridge, I noticed a black-clad figure down on the rocks by the water. As I got closer it became clear that it was a boy crouched by the lapping waves–only he was wearing a top-hat and tails; not some pristine rental costume but a ragged suit that had been well lived in. The "Artful Dodger" from *Oliver Twist* immediately came to mind. Once again, his attention was fixed on something or somewhere else. There's a scene in the film where Jack Dawkins encounters Oliver for the first time. He says to him: "What you starin' at? Haven't you never seen a toff?" I was half expecting the fellow down below to turn around and say something similar to me. "My eyes! How green can you get?"

Not only does your focus of attention–your beliefs about yourself; what you are, where you are going; your understanding of the mechanisms of your existence–matter to you in daily living, but it can affect what happens to you afterwords. The dogmatic religions reduce life to the binary opposition of good and evil; heaven and hell, but it is my belief that the universe is essentially a benevolent construct, based on well being. It wouldn't be much of a system if it wasn't based on free will–therefore expressing a desire or orientation for something is inclined to bring it your way sooner or later. The word manifestation has been used already, and is the crux of most arguments, "scientific" or "metaphysical".

Life can trick you into thinking you are powerless and stuck in poverty or a class system or undesirable social milieu. The self-deceit can last even into death–the consciousness has become trapped, even if the "body" has long gone. You always know a ghost by the look in their eyes; they are not looking at you, but past you–into some unfathomable void of their own imagination.

Evolution might be likened to the development of vision; the myopia of the embattled, frustrated individual becomes lateral and encompassing, then eventually takes on great sweeping vistas, where the self is posited as part of something very big and very perfect–but first the layers of distortion and obstruction must be peeled away. The frame of that lens is what we know as the ego. The ferocity of the dogs at the kennel was not a little intimidating, but at least it was honest–they left little doubt about their intentions.

Must respect take the form of a trounced opponent? The "actualised", balanced man or woman feels no need to feed on the spurts of fear he or she elicits from an overbearing stance. The so-called yin and yang symbol would seem to be just that; one pursuant of the other–an aggressor and submissive; an animal chasing its prey; a husband and wife in court squabbling over the spoils of their marriage. What's the missing link? In ecclesiastical circles much gravitas is given to the Holy Trinity–the Father, Son and Holy Ghost–but what practical, metaphysical application can it have? Well, if the "source" is present and the other two elements are connected, then we have a trinity, and a symbiotic, organic triumvirate. It is self-sustaining, with no need for the troublesome ebb and flow of the former model–it is a love triangle in the highest sense.

With gender roles becoming more varied and indistinct, why settle for restriction? Who's to say the human consciousness can't identify with one facet of the great archetypal mind, or indeed blend and integrate aspects from both, becoming reflections of the highest orders of the heavens–to identify with the Mother, in her perfect, enigmatic form, and the Father in his expansive, utterly benevolent self?

When in doubt, go back to the basics: look to children as vessels of purity; borrow from their example, the simplicity and honesty of their interactions. Set your expectations high. The greatest beings I have encountered were child-like in their countenance; unbridled in their joy; infused with the security of self-belief.

A MAZE OF IDEAS

"What you are shouts so loudly in my ears I cannot hear what you say." Ralph Waldo Emerson

The New Age movement contains remnants of the old Vedic and Pagan belief systems that have survived the imposition of "rationality" on the scientific, cultural and political spheres. As anyone who has attended a workshop on spiritual matters or listened to any number of gurus will realise is that the gulf between the rational world and that of the esoteric is sometimes too far to bridge. The feelings of disappointment that brought the individual to seek alternative paradigms and explanations can become compounded as one bewildering premise is swapped for another. However, any compelling esoteric discourse will let itself be felt, even more than it can be intellectualised.

Some of those attracted to this milieu of competing and complimentary ideologies obviously feel shortchanged by the traditional religious and institutional systems. In the same way that some people end up idolising their pet animals as a substitute for disappointing personal relationships, the New Age pursuant can sometimes end up merely reconfiguring their own perceptual filters–or suspicions and distrust of others–in the context of the new terms of reference. They might say they are psychically sensitive, so don't want to get too close to ordinarily humans, and are only interested in the rarified presence of such and such a "spiritual leader", or that they have a special relationship with this or that "master" (in the non-physical realms)–and thereby justify their supercilious stance. For some, it becomes a journey into self-righteousness.

But the pursuit of purity–as understood or felt–requires a pure vessel. And that most often means separating the mechanisms of the ego from the higher Self.

I once gave a lift to a friend who wanted to visit a shaman out in the Somerset countryside. She was a very knowledgeable and intuitive person, but I was not sure she really believed what she had heard preached–about manifestation, for example. We were driving back to London late in the evening and I remarked that I longed to gaze upon an open fire once more. Shortly afterwards we stopped at a country pub (interestingly called the Angel Inn) for a bite to eat. On entering through the medieval door we were greeted by the sight of a huge log fire, embracing the room with its warm glow. After dinner we returned to the car park. Opening the car door, I glanced up at the night sky, admiring the starry view afforded by the unlit countryside. I made a throwaway remark about being better able to spot UFOs, of which my friend made light by shaking her head. I then asked her if she would like to see a space ship, to which she replied in jocular, dismissive fashion. We were no sooner on our way, when the car's GPS sent us down a narrow country lane, flanked by a thick hedge on one side and open fields on the other. I began to worry that if we were met by a car coming in the other direction we wouldn't be able to manoeuvre backwards. But it wasn't the road from which the traffic came, but the sky. To my right, out of the gloom, swooped a glowing green triangular "craft" that momentarily trailed alongside the car and then veered off suddenly to disappear from sight. I looked at my passenger, who was agog and now suddenly lost for glib repostes. Sometimes it does take a direct experience of the unknown to break through the barrier of inner disbelief. Much lip service is paid to the power of the imagination–or, more specifically, ideas–but it is belief that thrusts those ideas into manifest form.

Most of us have a reserve of politeness and consideration that we access in social interactions. But if it is just an act, then there comes a time when it's curtains up. A friend who recently returned from a three-week trip to China recounted how his hosts at a journalism college made every effort to speak in English, include him in social activities and even share their food. Towards the end of the third week, as he sat down to breakfast in the communal fashion, his continuing awkwardness with chopsticks seemed to puncture the bubble of inclusiveness. This was not so much expressed, as felt, he said.

The ritual of courtship is one such example; scrubbed clean, groomed, wearing our best finery, and smelling like a field of Gardenias in full bloom, we set out to win over the prospective mate. But how often do we dismiss out of hand the initial impulse–that wordless insight–we receive at the moment we encounter that person for the first time? It is more faint than the clamour of our desires and seems to arrive using a different entry point to our normal thoughts, so we distrust it; it is not of ourself, we say. But that intuition–not just a gut feeling–is most usually the voice of wisdom from the bigger Self. Instead the social pressure to score a success in the dating game or the chronological, biological imperative to "settle down" or the looming spectre of loneliness justify the compromises and "practical" considerations. I have both celebrated in relief at having listened to it and recanted in agony at having ignored it. What a shortcut to success, if we would only heed it–and, better still, cultivate it.

During my late teens I visited an island off the west coast of Scotland with some friends. It made a welcome change from hanging around a pub, though with a circumference barely more than 10 miles this pretty little rock's charms soon wore off. As we stood waiting for the ferry back to the mainland, I wandered over to a raised bank on the other side of the road. There stood a huge bronze statue on a granite plinth. I gazed up at the face of a woman–her hair was tied in a bob and she sported the hooped skirt commonly worn in the Georgian era. I nearly fell to my knees as a flood of recognition and devotion overwhelmed my mind; I could barely breathe as a tangible emotion filled the air around me; what a fathomless respect I felt for this person and longed with all of my being to be by her side. Talk about agony and ecstasy; why must I be afflicted with this knowledge now, I wondered–a penniless, disenfranchised youth with little mobility or hope now granted a vision of what could only be out of his reach. The siren of the approaching boat was almost a relief; the doorway back to the safety of mediocrity and blandness. I sat on the ferry in a stupor of both bliss and regret–why hadn't I read what was written on the plaque, so that at least I could later investigate the origins of this memorial? My waking life up to that point had been a fog of indifference; the closest I'd come to a romantic liaison was sharing a cigarette with a female classmate. Now the full scope of human earthly love had materialised and landed on my lap. How to integrate this reality with the existing one? Mmm, better put it to one side for now, I concluded.

Some time later, and with some reticence, I contacted the local tourist office and enquired about the large bronze statue overlooking the ferry terminal. At last, the name of this figure would be revealed, and perhaps eventually my connection to her. After providing a careful description of the location and object over the phone, the friendly but perplexed official replied: "But there are no statues on the island."

To be honest, I had had intimations of this force at other times, but they had been easier to disengage from. Most had been at night, on journeys that approximated dreams but were far more visceral and lucid. These waking transmigrations always take place when I would least expect them; in fact, most often when my state of mind is ambivalent or focused on material banalities. Perhaps that is there purpose, to act as reminders of a greater truth that punctuate the otherwise merciless ritual of life.

Once, as a twelve-year-old sitting in class, I ventured into my pencil case for an eraser and came across a small pendant with the face of Jesus. Perhaps my mother had placed it there for luck. As I held it in my hand, a soft warmth began to grow; like holding a light bulb that has just been switched on, only this did not burn. Its glowing warmth slowly moved up my arm and I began to feel a serenity and dislocation from the room. I flinched, and dropped the pendant. Crickey! What will the teacher say if I don't finish these sums, urged my ego mind.

Jesus for many of us is the epitome of human achievement; we reach for his image in our minds whenever trouble looms; he is the ultimate archetypal refuge for the physically focused human. And yet how that ideal has been used to overshadow us with a latent, unjustified sense of guilt–the personification of God who was executed in order to absolve humanity for its ignorance and wretchedness. The abstract theological musings on his perfection leave us little room to interpret his tangible example to others–why even try when you sinners are so far from his grace anyway, goes the implication.

We have been conditioned to believe that suffering is the only real way to evolve. The collective mind has been subject to this bondage for millennia. But personal development, growth and enlightenment can be the consequence of a joyous, creative existence too; in fact it is a more efficient way to learn, allowing a more energised and dynamic life, without the weighty byproduct of emotional baggage that comes with strife. What on television is termed drama is all too commonly hysterics and neurosis. Time to change that well worn script.

Our lives have been bookended by the "pain of birth" and the "pain of death", but it needn't be so–both are transitions from one place to another; just like a summer holiday, the coming and going can be relished with the same excitement. Change your beliefs and you change your experience–as the mind begets matter.

We have a tendency to become apathetic when unchallenged; and pain serves as an impetus to action. But you can avoid the "pain" if you have the discipline to remember and re-enact those states of mind that necessity precipitates in times of crisis.

My reaching drinking age coincided with the advent of the superpub–vast, showy hybrids of the night club and bar with heady, energetic music. This more dynamic social milieu was an exciting departure from the staid public houses that proliferated at the time. However to enter that realm was to pit your fashion credentials and street cred against the coolest folks in town. One night, after borrowing my brother's jeans and his new T-shirt, I perched myself near the edge of the long bar and took in the scene. Two bronzed and trendy Adonises supped their beer nearby. As I began to ponder my contrasting pale complexion and thin frame, my eyes fixed on a stunning ash blond woman gliding along the far side of the balustrade. Her eyes held me firmly in place; the normal polite deferral of gaze did not apply here; something was being communicated invisibly but compellingly. She moved closer, negotiating the busy throng of people without looking away or diverging from her track. Once again, an otherworldly haze began to descend; to be beheld by this person was to be regarded with the highest esteem, uplifted to greatness. The intense stare emanated a tremendous maturity and self-respect. While everybody else wore casual garb of chinos, shirts and tight dresses, this majestic apparition was clothed in a white frilly blouse and checked sports blazer, as if she had just stepped off an aristocratic estate from the early 20th century. Nobody else gave her a second glance. As she drew nearer, so the intensity of her presence increased, as if her utmost regard was funnelled into a beam that was directed at my body. How could a stranger summon such regal intent towards another person? If it went on much longer, I felt I would explode. She passed behind the two men at my side and I turned expecting to meet her at my back–but, no, she was gone.

The pain of separation was searing; the glow of the bar now dim and superficial.

This would not be the only time my thoughts of self-doubt were met by an immediate and profound encounter in the visual realm. On the day I started work at a well known business newspaper in London I was standing at the train station in Greenwich, having decided to leave the bike at home. A scattering of people dotted the platform, though they all appeared stalk still–perhaps, I assumed, comatose at the thought of venturing into the city. Or was it some trepidation faced by the presence of a giant among their number? Though no one turned to look, a man about seven or eight feet tall began to wind his away along the platform in my direction. He was almost African, but not quite, and his tremendous height did not look inappropriate to his wiry, powerful frame. Before I knew it he was standing before me; I gazed up at his face and felt the immediate reassurance of being in the company of a wise and benevolent personality–despite the casual garb of jeans and T-shirt. He said something to the effect: "They don't know what we know, do they?", then, after a pause: "No FT, no comment." I barely noticed him leave, as I tried to digest his words, and figure out how he could know my destination. I never did make sense of it, of course. What elevated the experience to new realms was, once again, the visitor's sense of presence–where the people around me were neither here nor there, caught in their own thoughts, not fully aware of themselves, this man presented himself in totality; I could feel his self-respect, and thus his respect for me–what it must be like to be regarded by a great king, if such a thing exists. The surroundings and any other thoughts became diminished while I was under the gaze of this regal consciousness. When the spiritual community talks about self-realisation, perhaps this is what they mean–a realness and presence that makes other people and objects seem like a faint mist in a dreamy world.

This stranger at the station knew himself, and therefore somehow knew me; that was the tangible feeling–a respect and love communicated by physical proximity and of a kind that you could say was wholly mature; grown-up; benevolent without being compromised. Everyone else I met that day–the people on the train; my new colleagues–were mere simulacrums in comparison.

It would not be an exaggeration to state that many people have never encountered "love" from another person–not from their parents, siblings or contemporaries. They blindly and doggedly follow the oblique rules and conventions of society, trusting that there will be some emotional pay-off somewhere along the line. They don't feel entirely whole or worthy but hope that out there somewhere awaits another individual, ready to fill in the missing links, providing some compensatory sustenance to their incompleteness.

When we reach adolescence we begin seeking relationships with the opposite sex, or the same sex depending on our orientation. Some of us hold high ideals of love, perhaps engendered by reading Mills and Boon, while others are happy to seek mere convenience. After all, if we have never been the subject of unconditional regard, why should we expect anything more in this context? We get together with a partner but don't really know what to expect. Will he or she love me more than I do them? Should I put up with his or her mood swings and laziness because that's the way my mother or father behaved? If we are not convinced of our own self-worth, then how do we know what is enough respect and what constitutes disrespect?

It has to be said that to encounter another person who reflects back at you some of your own tendencies and attributes can be a precious opportunity for self-realisation and "growth". As someone once said, we are permitted to walk with those who would show us ourselves. Though it goes without saying that it takes a commitment and disciplined effort to daily examine your motives and thoughts–including the historical landscape that has shaped your perceptions and expectations.

One way to reconfigure your outlook is to consider your eyes as projectors of your reality rather then receivers of it. There are children going through the schooling system now who seem to be unsettled and disruptive; the psychologists and medical establishment label them as having attention deficit hyperactivity disorder. It's interesting how any challenge to the status quo is always packaged or persecuted. The physicians and social scientists flood out like antibodies surrounding an invasive virus. If that fails, the apparatus of the chemical industry is rolled out, and then finally the "judicial" system. If the commonly accepted paradigms are so full-proof, then why do they strike discord in so many?

These children are admittedly subject to increasing amounts of synthetic compounds in their diets: the supermarkets are practically giving away "family packs" of fizzy drinks, crisps and chocolate bars; the pre-packaged meals that some parents feel obliged to use due to time constraints are denatured and chemical laden. And if any nutrients manage to survive that ordeal, we finish them off in a microwave oven. But above and beyond that, maybe these youngsters are just bored and patronised. I know I certainly was at school. Maybe the half-truths and demand for homogeneity just doesn't sit easily with beings who are more psychically aware than their predecessors.

The point is that these people are attempting to think for themselves; to challenge the orthodoxy, albeit in a physical, vocal and seemingly incoherent manner. Perhaps their teachers would have an easier time if they adopted a more lateral approach, even if the syllabus is not. Each year in India, Teachers' Day celebrates the bond between pupils and educators. In many schools the students will serve their teachers' meals, and then they will all eat together. It is a reciprocal respect that lays the ground work for a love of knowledge and learning–not so much what is said, but what is done.

My childhood and then early adolescence was akin to being tossed into the air on a giant spinning coin–on one side the mark of neglect and on the other the symbol of freedom–and where I would land was anyone's guess. The lack of structure to some extent meant a lack of dogma; the paradigm of the empowered individual would have to be one I discovered for myself.

The Dark Night of Soul for me began after the family home was sold and I began living alone. By the time I was 21, the discord between the values and principals fostered by cultivating an "internal life" and what I saw around me began to impinge on my sense of wellbeing. While at college, I remember turning up for work experience at an advertising agency and the account director's first utterance: "Geez, looks like you had a rough night." If I had told him that I'd had barely a wink of sleep in seven months, he might have sent me home. My pillow obviously didn't have a silver lining but the overall experience did–and it took the form of meditation. My sister, one day noticing my zombie state, foisted a Yellow Pages into my hand and pointed to a listing for Transcendental Meditation. I obeyed the good advice and turned up at their next induction. On the second day of practising TM my sleep worries were over and a new vista of tranquility had unfolded.

It would not be an exaggeration to say this technique has saved my life; it sustains me physically through the rigours of daily life and has laid the foundation for greater insight. On about the third day of this new routine, I found myself staring down at a plate of chicken jalfrezi, ordinarily a treasured feast, but now the lumps of meat seemed alien and unpalatable. Some internal shift had triggered a physical rejection of meat; only a vegetarian, and better still a vegan, diet would do. For me, the meditation process is not akin to sleep or even rest, but most usually involves a complete shutdown of the body and senses; to return from this state is to reinhabit a lifeless body, scarcely even breathing.

In the twenty years I have been meditating, I have occasionally glimpsed other realms while on the cusp of returning to wakefulness. On one occasion, in the fraction of a second between awareness and full lucidity, I held the answer to every question I could imagine, as if falling into a zone where all knowledge resided, where everything was clear and unhindered. I clung to this prize data as my mind unfolded it usual systems, but just glimpsing the light of the room was enough to blast its detail out of mind. Perhaps the brain just wasn't equipped to hold it.

The transcendent experience is often ineffable–at least in this language, which was primarily designed to facilitate the trade of material goods–but that is not reason enough to dismiss it.

Once, over the period of a week, as I closed my eyes I would see the most grotesque faces on the back of my eyelids–human-like and not so human-like. There was no fear or emotion, just observation. This is also the gift of meditation–the perspective to view the polarised forces at work in the world and accept their right to exist. For those who have had their emotional and mental development stunted or warped by their life's antagonisms, the meditative state can provide a backdoor to realms where "maturity" pervades all–and this mindset can then, either immediately or over time, be integrated into the waking personality. To get out of yourself is very often to discover yourself–as you might discover an exquisitely beautiful garden on an unplanned day trip.

A friend brought back a souvenir from Brazil; a small pyramid-shaped piece of quartz. The day she had bought it, there had been a spectacular thunder storm. I was always receptive to such accounts as I had enjoyed these heavenly displays as a child in western Canada. The following day, I sat down to meditate with the crystal in my hand–and had an impulse to stick it to my forehead. I closed my eyes and immediately there was a blinding flash–a blanket of white momentarily replaced the dark red hue of my eyelids–then there was a crack and rumble of thunder right above my head that shook the concrete foundations and rattled the windows in their hinges. After a second or two there was another crack, this time less severe. Far from feeling shocked, I felt elated at the release of unbridled raw power. Expecting to see a darkened sky, I pulled back the curtains, only to gaze out at a serene, sunny day. Enquiring later of a neighbour if she had been caught out in the storm, I received merely a quizzical look in reply. The weather front had materialised inside my flat, not outside.

Of course, not everyone's experience of meditation is so visceral, but it shouldn't be ruled out.

The pervasive effect of technology has the opposite effect; it turns the individual's focus outwards towards its superficial stimuli. We become preoccupied with someone else's agenda–dictated by the architecture of our "time-saving" devices. The valuable process of self-reflection is now absent from many people's lives; ask them a question about themselves and they look blank or just recite a cliche picked up from television. The life of constant distraction risks becoming a mere fantasy dictated and directed by others.

The proliferation of outlets for "ideas" could be a great boon for popular culture; the increased reach afforded by a multitude of television channels, smartphones and tablet devices has also provided more opportunities to monetise content. But look at that content–shallow, vapid, formulaic. It seems the slashed economies of production and speed of execution have added to the dispersal of energy–quality has been sacrificed for quantity.

The narrative of the mundane dulls our wits while celebrities are churned out before our judgmental gaze; only those who elicit a self-effacing worship or earn our scorn endure beyond the obligatory 15 minutes.

The level of media noise has increased but the amount of information made available has diminished. One might perceive an agenda of instigating mental poverty among the masses. And it seems we are all kept so busy–so distracted–that we are scarcely able to notice the bigger picture or to ask the big question–where are we going as a society?

HIGH SOCIETY

As humans we have an inherent ability to literally get out of our body; in an act of imagination, you could take your awareness to the corner of the room and view yourself where you sit or stand. Every time someone approaches me with some "juicy gossip" about another person or launches into a diatribe about some sorry state of affairs, I would like to be able to lift us both up, about ten feet in the air, and let that person view themselves set in that broader landscape. If you momentarily put yourself into the shoes of the individual you are aggrieved by it will provide a valuable counterweight to the impending onslaught. To keep bad company is to be led astray–and those who take pleasure in other people's misfortune or who seek to undermine another's sovereignty carry a plague that is deadly to the spirit.

That an individual has been born, acclimatised to being in a body; who has been through the often absurd educational system; who exerts the discipline to get up every morning, who must reconcile all the dangers and impositions that state and society says exist; who is obliged to breathe, eat, defecate, deal with illness, the rigours of work–does that alone not make them worthy of the deepest respect? Why seek to add more burdens by thinking ill of them or wishing them harm? How many intelligent, perceptive people have I come across who spend most of their energy being irritated by those who cannot live up to their "standards"–an irritation borne of their own attributes manifest in others. They hold themselves in a hyper-critical, judgmental state–which risks eventually turning them into that which they despise. What a waste of a life.

In recent years a sociological phenomenon has begun to manifest before my eyes. Quite often, while going to pay a bill at a restaurant or at the counter of a sandwich bar the person serving me will refuse to take my money or will discretely figure in a discount. It doesn't happen every time, but enough to warrant consideration, and for anybody with me to enquire, "why do they do that to you?" After 40 years of meeting and dealing with all types of people and simultaneously being privy to the wider non-physical facets of life, it has become habitual for me to look beyond surface personalities and to consider each individual as being merely a reflection of something much grander–in other words, to perceive a Soul standing before me, rather than just an individuated ego-complex. That Soul may in turn reach out with a gracious gesture, such as a "freebie" or other act of kindness. That glimmer of recognition is most apparent in their eyes, as if someone else were suddenly peering out and smiling. I mention eateries as a common example but this exchange has taken place at passport control, on public transport and every kind of retail outlet.

And it doesn't just happen with people.

It wasn't that long ago that I could drive down to the coast before work and take a swim in the sea before starting an evening shift in the office. On one such occasion, I had gotten up very early on a sunny morning and headed off in my car to a beautiful cove outside Cork city. The sun was still low in the sky as I set off on foot across the clipped fields that traced the line of the coast. Up ahead, blocking the only exit in an otherwise impenetrable hedge, was a large white bull. He didn't look too pleased to see me brazenly cutting through his territory–and on course for a face-off. As I approached, he made one of those sudden turning movements that suggested he meant business. Perhaps he had been pushed around for too long by the farmer and decided to stand his ground. With no desire to cause offence, I hopped over the fence and made my way along the barbed wire. He wasn't for moving though. There was a path of sorts leading down the cliff edge and onto an inlet where the rock had been eaten away by the sea. The tide was out, so I ventured down. To get over the other side would mean scaling the next piece of land jutting into the sea. Up I went, the first dozen steps easily supported by firm ground. I reached a small plateau and turned to look about; the tide was edging in, but I would soon be over the other side anyway. The last stretch was overhung with earth; I reached out to find a handle, but it crumbled in my hands. The danger now was that I could fall backwards if the soil gave way once I had pulled my weight onto it. The sun was beating down, and I didn't fancy becoming a cooked breakfast. Another try; this time further along. As my hand went up, a cacophony of noise erupted behind me; like a group of punters at the races decrying a losing horse. I could almost make out words in the verbal melee. Who or what was behind me? I edged around to find half a dozen black birds perched at eye level on the out-facing cliff. We viewed each other in silence. They were in control of their surroundings and I wasn't–and we all knew it. Again I grasped upwards, and again the verbal onslaught resumed. This was no sound I had ever heard from a bird; being closer to some eastern European language than chirping or tweeting. They were saying something and it wasn't an endorsement of my climbing ability. All I had to do was lift a hand and they would respond. Perhaps I should take their advice, but the sea was now lapping at the rocks below. In an experimental move, I lowered my leg to what seemed like a rock below; the ovation of chatter was immediate–and distinctly different. They were almost cooing in support of this new strategy, but again in no harmonic spectrum I would have associated with birds. My right foot was on a secure ledge but my left foot was still up above, and I couldn't see where to put it. There was a gentle, giddy jabber from one of the birds which had a reassuring effect. I took a chance and pirouetted around on my right foot to face outwards with my feet now placed side by side. Nothing for it now but to jump... the crash into the sea sounded worse than it felt, but I was nonetheless soaked up to the waist. I saluted my new friends and made my way back up the path I'd come down.

In a more abstract but no less potent display, as I write these words a huge rainbow has appeared outside my window; a reminder of the multifarious and splendid dimensions usually just outside our spectral view. Rudolph Steiner[10], the Swiss educationalist, would surely agree that colour is integrally linked to the forces of the universe; it is "the soul of nature and the whole cosmos, and we participate in this soul when we experience colour".

The space of miracles is that created by high regard–or love–for another living being, where notions of selfish

10 Rudolf Steiner, Blackboard Drawings 1919-1924, Walter Kugler; Rudolf Steiner Press

genes or primordial urges dissipate and are replaced by the unlimited faculty of the Soul. Its physical form and nature takes on a hue that supplants the habitual, conditioned processes, and exclaims, "look who I am really!" The ordinary can become extraordinary under the sway of the Soul's master mind.

You know things are happening when you begin to get the answers just before you get the questions; and this is a consequence of a shift in orientation from "what can I get out of this situation?" to "what can I offer in this situation?" By extension, you might be walking down the street and overhear two people talking about the main players in the Mongolian government, and then come across a colleague on the way into the office who asks you if you know anything about Mongolian politics, as he or she is on their way to an interview for the job of foreign correspondent of the New York Times; you repeat what you have just heard–assuming it feels right–and both of you continue seamlessly onwards. At a more simplistic level, you will notice that more people stop you in the street to ask for directions–even in foreign countries. I'm sure a native stopped me in Beijing, the day after I arrived–even though I look like a Viking.

Having a benevolent personal resonance is not the same thing as having "MUG" tattooed onto your forehead–in fact, the victims and energetic leeches of this world run a mile when confronted with an individual embodying self respect. Of course, it is that state which allows you to give without needing anything in return.

These are just indicators, but the synchronous scale can stretch all the way to the heavens.

Some years ago I flew into San Francisco airport, where the stream of passengers was directed into a vacuous hall divided by a bank of booths–manned by the sentries of passport control. It had been decades since I'd been in North America[11], and there was a noticeable change in the register of the collective mind, at least of the several thousand people in the airport. Not unlike those dystopian zombie films you chance upon late at night while flicking through the TV channels, the visual spectrum was of muted colours and a blue-grey haze–the ocular signature of both subjugation and submission. I had visited China–that cartoonish nightmare of statehood–but the underlying current of consciousness there was akin to a sleeping lion; it threatened to rear up at any moment and overwhelm its oppressors–and not necessarily in violence. (That collective realisation of inherent power needs only a meeting of the cognitive and spiritual cogs for transmission to take place, not unlike the clutch engaging the powertrain in a car.) Here, Aslan had been replaced by Bagpuss. Standing in line, it became clear that an Orwellian biometric scrutiny was awaiting the hundreds of people feeding into the customs booths. As I approached the terminal, a surge of revulsion ran through me, which was met by a determination to resist the imminent cataloging process. Just as I reached the operator, there was a lull in proceedings and a shout from the floor. The attendant asked me to wait, and a supervisor appeared and gave instructions to his colleagues. "Just show me your passport," came the

---

11 As a child living in Canada in the late 1970s, I witnessed (and felt) the emergence of a more dynamic creative and social autonomy–an assuredness about the benefits of diversity and original thought. This was apparent in the "vibe" that infused popular culture and fashion of the time but also in the ambience of collective thought. However, it was soon to be quenched by the unholy alliance of Ronald Reagan and Margaret Thatcher who, through their policies and example, realigned the masses with the basal instincts of greed and fear.

request. "Is that all?" I asked. "Yes, the system has gone down." Thank goodness, I thought.

It may have been a coincidence that a technicality spared me the indignity of being scanned and canned, but at least some resistance remained. If I had willingly subjected to the blanket imposition (which didn't exist the last time I was in North America), then perhaps fate–or psychic override–wouldn't have kicked in. If there was indeed some psychic faculty at work, then imagine how more pervasive it could be with everyone in that hall focused in the same manner. My objection was not some blasé ideological position; I REALLY DIDN'T WANT IT TO HAPPEN. Indeed, the point is not to meet force–in this case a stringent security process–with force but to enter a mental zone of personal sovereignty, where such a derogation becomes much less likely in your reality. I imagine Mahatma Gandhi demonstrated a similar approach in his dealings with the British, where an imperial power suddenly found itself impotent next to the realised nobility–or self-worth–of one individual.

Some of the most dynamic human catalysts in history achieved the most by being the most "inactive"–many of whom came and went unnoticed.

There is a distinction to be made here, in case it wasn't obvious. In my experience, there are serious repercussions for the wanton use of psychic "power". The effects are wide-ranging and beyond analysis but inevitably find their way back to the originator. This may be why those who have famously dabbled in black arts–think of Aleister Crowley[12]–have led lives marked by tragedy.

---

12 Edward Alexander Crowley (1875-1947) was an English magician and alchemist who became associated with diabolism and ritualised sex.

Those who embark on that road are heading in a very different direction from the likes of Gandhi–and will require nothing less than the grace of God to rescue them from their energetic convolutions.

It might be said that he explored his potent occult faculties in the pursuit of fame but also out of rebellion against a puritanical mother. A heroin addict and later alcoholic, he travelled the world, gaining notoriety for his unorthodox lifestyle and coterie of mistresses and apostles.

THE DANCE OF LIFE

After coming in late one night, I caught a performance on TV of *Chic* playing at the Glastonbury festival; how charismatic and eloquent were the duo of female singers; how dynamic the interplay of sax, guitar and drums; and of course underpinning it all the harmonious genius of composer Nile Rodgers. If extraterrestrials had been looking down on this concert they must have momentarily forgotten our foibles amid such a display of human sassiness and funkiness. Indeed, we should not neglect to acknowledge our own individual and collective brilliance–at least in terms of putting on a show.

Then again, all the acts that perform at the Glastonbury festival take on a magic hue–something of the pagan remains in the air and in the land. You might say that that special place has hidden depths, which literally resonate with some of us. Great musicians and performers are our modern day shamans; perhaps that is why this small spot on the globe has become a mecca for the world's great music makers–who are subconsciously driven there to pay homage to the invisible inspiration that has shaped their lives?

For my seventh birthday, my parents gave me a *10th anniversary James Bond Album Superpak* with John

Barry's full scoring for all the films up to *Diamonds are Forever*. I had been mesmerised by the incidental music from these movies even as a toddler, they told me, and from the first time I placed the needle on the vinyl to this day I have treasured that exquisite bundle of plastic and cardboard. Barry's scoring had a life of its own–it spoke to the action on the screen but also provided a subtext that, to me, beckoned us to a world of sublime dynamism. Bond danced in tune with the exotic locations and thereby was granted immunity from folly and harm. His–and our–enchantment would not have been possible without these sophisticated, transcendental melodies. Some of the 007 posters featured depictions of James Bond levitating with arms crossed like some medieval knight rising from the dead, the twinkle in eyes and subtle smirk reminiscent of the Mona Lisa–a secret agent with secret knowledge about his place in the world.

Needless to say, there are many more such examples in the spheres of music and culture.

CHINESE WHISPERS

The teachings of Confucius (551–479 BC) permeate the consciousness of modern China–at least at face value. When I was last in Beijing, 10 years ago, the city had a transitory population of 10 million people, who would wend their way through congested roads and narrow *hutongs* each day to get to work. The trains and bike lanes might have been filled to capacity, but not once did I encounter aggression or discourtesy. In fact, one gentleman broke with the throng to offer me directions to my hotel, actually walking half a mile out of his way to make sure I got there. This was one of the philosopher's Golden Rules in action–do unto others as you would have done unto you. Confucius also placed the family unit at the centre of his system–loyalty to parents, ancestor worship, respect for elders–even as the basis for a sound government. However, to visit a public convenience in China is to realise that in a general sense the populace have adopted his proclamation to the extent that the public space has become nobody's responsibility.

The more modern Chinese communist view posits that the collective good supersedes the demands of the individual; thus you have a huge compliant workforce. And yet it is no secret that they also have a small group of families–tied to the umbrella of the politburo structure–which controls much of the industry and commerce of the country.

So, once again, the machinations of the individual will–albeit a myopic, immature, embattled self–holds forth amid the specious dogma of a "collective" project. The most visible manifestation of this small-minded approach is the widespread pollution of air, land and water, on a holocaustic scale that threatens to burst even the controlling elite's private bubbles.

Likewise, in the west, the governments and banks readily quote the moral economic theories of Adam Smith to justify their aggregation of wealth–though Smith's classical free market economy was not configured around manipulation of inter-banking lending rates, foreign exchange rates, interest rates (driving small investors into property or equity bubbles), or inflated economic growth fuelled by unsustainable government borrowing. It is not Smith's moral prescriptions that have been adopted wholesale but–more secretly–his prohibitions.[13]

---

13 Adam Smith (1723-1790) was a product of the Scottish Enlightenment and was best known for his book, An Inquiry Into The Nature and Causes of The Wealth of Nations, though he was most proud of The Theory of Moral Sentiments, where he proposes a theory of sympathy, in which the act of observing others makes people aware of themselves and the morality of their own behaviour. His proposition that business helps others by helping itself was set in the context of a "free market"–based on natural incentives. Indeed, he demonstrated an awareness of this theory's fallibility when he warned of a possible "conspiracy against the public or in some other contrivance to raise prices". As far as he was concerned, a business-dominated political system would allow a conspiracy of businesses and industry against consumers, with the former scheming to influence politics and legislation. The British prime minister Margaret Thatcher was said to carry around a copy of The Wealth of Nations in her handbag.

Some "spiritual" adherents also carry this hallmark; the premise is "what can I do to evolve; where can I go with my spirituality; or commonly these days, "how is my ascension coming along?" But what if the question was– with genuine inquiry and resolve–what can we achieve as a community, or as a society, or as a civilisation? Do not the benefits of synergy apply here, and the adage, "many hands make light work"?

CLAN WARFARE

Shortly after moving to Scotland from Canada, one of the local kids invited me round to his house to watch a rental video. We must have been about nine or ten years old. I was used to the relaxed, neighbourly hospitality of Canadians, so it was nice to receive such a friendly welcome from his mother and older brother. We all sat down to watch the movie with tea and biscuits. Not long after the opening credits had run, there was a thundering sound from upstairs; it grew louder, until a large, muscular, hairy man appeared around the hallway door wearing only his underpants. He immediately flew at the older brother sitting on the couch opposite and jumped on top of him, unleashing a litany of kicks and punches mixed with expletives. Then, almost as quickly, he disappeared back up the stairwell. Nobody seemed particularly surprised, but perhaps sensing my disquiet, the mother calmly asked: "Another biscuit, James?" I had lost my appetite … and hoped the film would not be a violent one!

No doubt the father was meting out some retribution for a perceived wrong, but he also appeared to be exorcising his own pent up frustrations in the only way he knew how. How many generations of his family had passed on this poison chalice and how many more would learn to accept this behaviour as normal?

I would learn quite quickly that this society carried an undercurrent of anger; youthful ventures into the city centre were akin to a game of Russian roulette; you never knew who you were going to encounter at the next street corner–who might take offence at your face. The degree of simmering resentment appeared to be directly linked to the person's loquacity–the ability to express and assert themselves in daily interactions.

I developed a resolve not to tolerate any nonsense from people, and that unspoken commitment communicated itself through gesture and stance. The shield I erected worked at distancing me from the hostiles but also must have kept at arm's length more gentle souls who could have brought balance to that perspective. Later in life, while on holiday in Spain, I stumbled upon a bull run on its way to the corrida. I took up a position by the fence and awaited the arrival of the "toros bravos". They soon galloped into sight, flanked by testosterone-fuelled youths. As one particularly fierce bull approached my position, the crowd behind me scattered–but I was left standing, unable to back off. I would face down this brute no matter what; cowardice was not an option. The animal raked the fence violently with its horns and then cast its eyes in my direction: I could only admire its nobility and poise amid this charade of youthful ex-uberance. It must have been so surprised at not eliciting fear that it gave a proud roar and then sauntered on its way. On another occasion, while diving off an island in the Pacific, I became the focus of a curious barracuda. It circled me repeatedly, getting closer with each sweep. I eventually made eye contact with it and mouthed:

"What the heck are you looking at?" It retreated into the depths.

The risk with this brick-wall approach to social interaction is that it tends to make mountains out of mole hills. A heated but momentary exchange with another motorist or a disagreement with a spouse becomes a do-or-die scenario, rather than a mere exchange of views.

The warrior is nothing without wisdom; a reactive, untempered force is at the mercy of the elements, and other forces. Power–physical or otherwise–is best wielded by the wise. One noble knight from the Middle Ages was asked by his squire why he put so much effort into his attire before battle. He replied that he dressed so ornately in the hope that there would be no battle. His regalia would have projected status and power, but also beauty. The sheathed sword serves its owner well.

It is noteworthy that people who experience a benevolent, nurturing environment as children seem to go through life with far fewer antagonisms, as they have not been obliged to take up either a victim or defensive identity. The person walking down the street with a certain swagger or an aggressive dog by their side has merely donned a cloak of fearlessness; what insecurities lie beneath?

To encounter the person imbued with self-belief can be like peering into a parallel reality–they may be unremarkable looking and even irritatingly eccentric but events just fall into place for them. How many unlikely Lotharios did I encounter during my school years who had the personality and appearance of an inverted bin lid but who still had a magnetic effect on the opposite sex, and who cruised through life with enough money, friends and interests to keep them content. It is not to say that such people have necessarily reached the pinnacle of human evolution, but what does it matter if they can glide through life within the terms of their own imaginations?

BODY OF PROOF

The term "Christ" is most often used to refer to an individual who distinguished himself while living in Galilee some 2,000 years ago. But the "christed" state is available to anyone. To be the christ is just that, to embody that archetypal energy, with its myriad permutations–but ultimately embodying respect for the sovereignty of all other beings. Like the ancients who sculpted statues to embody their saints and deities, so too can an individual use his or her body as a more complete vessel for their Soul.

To embody such an attribute, or archetype, is to literally become a facet of "God"–the patriarchal or maternal countenance at the highest level. To know is to become; to understand is not enough. The archetypal makeup of God could be distinguished in several ways (for example, the Tarot lists 22 from its Major Arcana; Hinduism personifies at least seven), though to focus on two–the Mother and Father–is to cover many bases.

Therefore, for a father to view his child or partner, or colleague with that pure regard is for them also to realise "God" through him. Thus so for the mother–with her manifest attributes. Indeed, these aspects of the Father or Mother are not mutually exclusive to just men on the one hand and women on the other; both are available simultaneously or at different times. Transcending gender stereotypes is the least you can do in a limitless universe.

When someone says, "Oh, that swami had such a wonderful energy," or "I feel so at peace in this temple," it is, I would suggest, the tangible experience of being bathed in that archetypal presence. It is also manifest in physical characteristics; the face; the mouth; the eyes–providing an instant facelift in some cases.

NOW WHAT?

A child is born into this world from another. It surveys this new landscape and wonders what the rules are. The smell and touch of its mother is reassuring; it begins to identify with her and seeks to borrow from her paradigm of existence; her outlook becomes temporarily its outlook–if she is distrustful of others, it becomes distrustful; if she is neurotic, it becomes infected with this condition; if she is calm and at peace, so is the child. As soon as the umbilical cord is cut, other energetic cords take shape. Just like the physical organ connecting them, these invisible bonds are meant to be temporary lifelines. To become an independent, and then hopefully interdependent, individual requires an eventual severing of ties, so that the child-like relationship is cast off and the adolescent can flourish on their own terms. That means also reinterpreting the relationship between parent and child; no longer should it be the unbalanced one of instructor and pupil; the parents have much to learn from this representative of a new generation, with its receptors more acutely aligned with the developing collective thought. Humility and respect are required by both parents and offspring for this type of relationship to truly flourish.

For too long, men have been banished to the sidelines or sequestered to deal with the "practical" considerations of money-making and maintenance. Both the weight of responsibility and unbridled power foisted on women has fed a neurosis in some quarters and fostered a stifling dynamic where the child is not so much nurtured as held captive in the grip of a wilful and vampirish personality. This is one area where I hold forth, and what I say goes, is the unspoken mantra. It is most often not even a conscious behaviour but nonetheless provides a shot of energetic sustenance each time it is indulged. Men have been told for generations that they are not suited to childcare, but I know of many exceptions to this, where circumstance has foisted the man to the fore. Their unfussy pragmatism, creativity and delight in simple pleasures are a perfect ruse to the modern female's tendency to mendacity and subterfuge.

The demands of male-dominated industry and commerce have largely dictated the terms of these interactions between mother, father and child. Isn't it time the promise of technology was fulfilled and used to free up time and import flexibility for both parents to take equal roles with their offspring?

Our commercial taskmasters have convinced us that our identity lies in the job we do; to know thy place within the corporate structure is to feel grounded; what power is to be derived from the ability to earn and provide for others. How often, though, do men come to the end of their lives and wonder aloud about the substance of their flight through the world of work and the missed opportunities to engage with their family and friends on *their* terms? Not unlike a battery that has been concealed in a compartment for its usable life and is only released when it becomes a spent force.

Even a cursory glance at a graph plotting productivity gains over average mean incomes is very revealing.[14] In recent years there has been a divergence in the plot lines, and no prizes for guessing which one is going up. This means that the owners of capital are getting an ever larger share of GDP. Profits are rising much faster than wages, and the highest earners are getting a disproportionate increase versus the rest of the labour force. Not only is there a larger gap in "equality" but also a polarisation of the haves and have-nots–with possible attendant effects on social stability.

Newspaper offices have never been considered that last word in ergonomics, but in the old days, at least, they had a buzz and a certain dynamism. I have been in and around them from an early age; often watching my sub-editor father turning 800 words of verbiage into 300 words of sublime prose to a soundtrack of clanking typewriters and ringing phones. Those crude mechanics have been consigned to museums, and instead the virtual world of desk-top publishing has ushered in a streamlined, hushed and regimented sphere where the 24-hour churn of digital "news" leaves little space for post-deadline rest bites. With repartee held in check and all attention focused on the screen, one could be forgiven for thinking that the binary world of the computer has co-opted and mutated the material/biological space; the overexposed fluorescent lighting creates a monochromatic hyperreality where one's increasingly muted colleagues become reduced to mere simulacra. The contents of the pixelated VDU screen are never more than fuzzy, somewhat indistinct, representations. If, as once might have happened, the operator was to drift off into sleep–per chance to dream–they would inhabit a more

---

14 www.houseofdebt.org–The Most Important Economic Chart

visceral and lucid reality. The register of the office has been reduced to the binary–to black and white; an oppressive glare upon your darker clothes. Like many other such environments, there are less people to do more work–administered from the cyber domain in the shape of emails from managers or human resources departments. It is a reductionist world and perhaps the most vapid that we can experience.

It may get worse before it gets better, but then perhaps that is what is required to motivate and mobilise self-reflection on a societal scale–as no fundamental change will be effected until that happens.

There can be a noticeable change in a person's demeanour and outlook when one or both parents die; for some it is the start of a very long mourning that lasts the rest of their lives; for others it offers a liberation after invisible cords are finally severed. Neither scenario seems intrinsically healthy to me and both trace their roots back to the early days–or formative paradigm–of childhood.

We are shaped by the various tiers of architecture we inhabit: those of social society, technology, and institutions to name but a few–but there exist other realms and facets of the self that hold grander designs. Even a cursory examination of life processes suggests a cyclical nature underpinning everything; whether it be the seven-year cellular renewal of the body or the 26,000-year precession of the equinoxes. According to some metaphysical and opened-minded scientific schools we have reached the end of a 25,920-year cycle–more commonly associated with Mayan and Sumerian calendars. This derivative, "master" number is one of many that can be found in predictable patterns and recurrences throughout micro-scopic and macro-scopic life–as above, so below. Compare the elliptical nature of a shell to the spirals of a galaxy. That would suggest the presence of a guiding intelligence, and helps to reconcile the apparent paradox of order amid chaos. It's not that there is any imposition on free will, but rather that an individual's or collective's desires and expression are given a structure within which to incrementally work back towards their source–or indeed move further away from it. Some individuals might choose to repeat the same processes over and over; and who's to say they shouldn't or couldn't?

This "new age" discourse proposes that the Earth, having progressed in its own evolution, will now ascend to a higher vibratory realm, leaving behind the more dense facets of its being. Those people on the planet who have similarly refined their energy, through purer thoughts and actions, will continue on that path along with the planet, while those individuals who have remained in the denser mindset of greed, envy and selfishness will remain with the old Earth, to repeat the cycle once more.

As of December 29, 2012, we officially entered the Golden Age foretold for thousands of years. Rejoice! Merriment!–even if you don't believe it, and let its positive emotional quotient outweigh the gloom of the Armageddonites.

A while back, as I was driving through Wiltshire, a huge crop circle loomed as I turned a corner; it was a yin and yang symbol. I asked a knowledgable Vietnamese friend what he thought it meant. "Ah!" he scratched his head, "the whole universe is being realigned, so the large dark portion is being relegated to the small black spot."

"Oh, I see," I said, scratching my head.

The only imperative to transcend the current layer of reality should come from self discovery; the delight in realising that more refined consciousness exists just outside of this visible light spectrum and that it can be engaged at will. A range of archetypal templates are also accessible, which can be used as guidelines or aspirations. Mediation is one useful tool for quieting the mind and embracing the inherent wisdom of silence, but once you begin to entertain the idea that God speaks through many channels, every object, interaction and experience can become your teacher and guide. The ancient tradition of Kriya yoga–espoused by Paramahansa Yogananda–also provides specific and ingenious techniques for gradually realising the internalised God.

I hear people increasingly refer to "synchronicities" in their lives–encountering double numbers on their digital clocks with uncommon regularity or asking a question and then having it immediately answered by a seemingly haphazard encounter or event.

Almost everyone I've heard mention ancient Egypt, does so in a tone of reverence. For me the idea that a pharaoh obliged thousands of people to sweat and toil their lives away building a monument to him or her was enough to neutralise any awe from its glittering artefacts (I don't now believe that the pyramids were built using slave labour or for egotistical indulgence). So, I have never given much thought to their deities or customs. At least until now. For some months I had been concerned about an aspect of my daughter's welfare, in the process enduring more than a few sleepless nights. Not living in the same household as her, I often covet the notion that I may one day be able to tuck her under the covers and read her bedtime stories. On the days we meet, she invariably greets me with an all-embracing hug. It is the greatest pleasure and honour to be able to return her warm affections–and so, in my absence, I one day imagined Mother God embracing and protecting her. Over the course of the following week something reached out–using the mundane incursions of everyday life to make itself known. As I sat down at my desk at the start of my working day, the woman beside me exclaimed, "Oh, I was in your neck of the woods at the weekend–at the Isis Inn." On the coach home, I glanced up from my slumber to catch the neon sign of a beauty salon called "Isis". The next day, while chatting with someone in their kitchen, I noticed the brand of his cooker–Isis. I awoke the following day to the sound of a parcel dropping through the letterbox. My brother had sent a newspaper cutting; my eye was drawn to the caption, which read: "…he was the editor of Isis magazine." On the road later, I passed a pick-up truck emblazoned with "Isis Rescue." Then there was a lorry with "Isis Removals." A day later, I found myself standing admiring a beautiful stone cottage in a quaint village; it had a burglar alarm–with simply "Isis" in capital letters. At the end of the week, in the early hours of the morning, my coach turned into the station, then halted suddenly. Outside, perfectly framed in my window, were the words "Isis Rescue" on the same tow truck, now parked alongside a broken-down bus. I took a book from the shelf as I headed to bed; opening it randomly, a sentence jumped out: "The Emperor Theodosius confiscated the property of 'heretics' and took over their temples. Statues of Isis were rededicated to Mary."

The first thing I did on Saturday was switch on my computer and do an internet search for this goddess, Isis.

The first paragraph in a listing on Wikipedia reads: "Isis (Original Egyptian pronunciation more likely "Aset" or "Iset") is a goddess in Ancient Egyptian religious beliefs, whose worship spread throughout the Greco-Roman world. She was worshipped as the ideal mother and wife as well as the patroness of nature and magic. She was the friend of slaves, sinners, artisans, the downtrodden, but she also listened to the prayers of the wealthy, maidens, aristocrats, and rulers. Isis is often depicted as the mother of Horus, the hawk-headed god of war and protection. Isis is also known as protector of the dead and goddess of children."

I may or may not yet discover the full extent of her intercessions, but who could not be grateful for the gracious and forthright introduction. A sense of powerlessness has been been diminished by a renewed sense of trust.

The urge to call out to the heavens for help when faced with frustration or trauma is perfectly natural–but when the instinct instead becomes one of "now, God, watch me transform this situation myself", then that is the mark of the self-possessed knower of thy self, and a true vote of confidence in God.

The phenomenon of synchronicities involves ingratiating and sometimes profound gestures, but for me there is little substitute for the recognition and activation of that wordless voice which resides in the higher Self, and which unfailingly dispenses the greatest treasures of wisdom–uniquely placed as it is to know all your past and future selves, and every molecule of your current self. The trick is to know it, and then listen to it–for it does not always follow the strictures of "rational" thought or logic. The perch whence it resides is way beyond that.

The dream state can also be a gateway to a more expansive perspective.

I was blessed to be able to spend three weeks on the Big Island of Hawaii a few years ago. The wildlife there have few if any predators and so, on sea or land, are approachable and inquisitive. Butterflies happily rest on your head, doves are not shy about sharing your picnic and manta rays will surface just to engage you on your terrain. On my first morning I raced down to the beach, ready to surmount the famous waves. As my car drew closer to the coastline, a rip current about four stories high banked on the beach and then suddenly broke. A couple of surfers seemed to ascend the next wave vertically on their boards, then surmount its tip, gliding back out to sea. My romantic notions from watching *Hawaii Five-0* evaporated in the sea spray. I would at least go for a swim, and hopefully circumvent the monster waves. It was not long before the breakers were behind me and the open ocean lay ahead. As a giant orange sun emerged beyond the horizon, a shoal of dolphins broke surface just feet away. What a bundle of auditory and kinetic delight: their banter of high-pitched tweets and whistles trumpeted the joy of camaraderie and physicality as they passed before me in leaps and bounds.

To witness such frivolity and unity placed these creatures in a higher order of being; a consciousness beyond the reach of dogma or platitudes. The "aloha" spirit began here, and I could imagine how the native population would have had little resistance to its charms.

While there someone told me a story about how a fisherman had returned to his nets, to find an entangled Great White shark. He cut it free and expected it to swim away; instead it circled his boat and gently nudged up against the bow. On his next trip out to check his nets, the shark was there waiting. It nestled beside his boat and he began to stroke it. The shark, far from being a mindless killer, behaved with gratitude and affection. They apparently maintain a close bond.

The existentialists, so erudite and precise in their pronouncements on humanity, need have looked no further than Nature for the answers to their philosophical dilemmas.

No long after returning from Hawaii, I had a dream-like encounter with a dolphin–an unusually pale one. As an outboard boat bobbed on the currents, I donned my flippers and oxygen mask. The pilot of the boat stood and watched as I slipped into the sea. A white dolphin seemed to appear out of nowhere; it nudged against me affectionately and we made eye contact; what a privilege to be so close to this elegant creature, I thought. It radiated a selfless compassion but also the composure of wisdom. The purity of its consciousness was tangible and intoxicating. It seemed to direct another beam of pure intent towards me and immediately my perspective shifted: I felt the analogous relationship between the sea and the cosmos–the mammals and fish swimming around in this invisible substrate were like all life in the universe, suspended by the binding and invisible substance of love.

Whether in the "dream" state or wakefulness, these encounters with such pure-intentioned beings are the most lucid and tangible I know. In comparison, there is something fuzzy and indistinct about the daily interactions we consider to be three dimensional. They say love endures, well, in my experience it transcends time and space. If only human interactions could also be this way–and in so doing become more real.

Keeping a journal is a wonderful way to build up a repository of wisdom delivered through your dreams that can be examined time and again. It also has the effect of disciplining the mind to remember these nightly encounters more vividly. The thing about dreams is that they are generally for and about you, and are rarely about what they're about–in other words don't take them at face value, look for the subtle meanings and cues and pay attention to the emotional volume too. We too often dismiss our nocturnal musings as abstract and unimportant workings of the subconscious, but they are no less facets of the imagination than is the waking state. While awake we are subject to the power of other people's ideas, by night it is our ideas that hold sway. To pay attention to your dreams is to pay attention to your Higher nature.

Some people will remain in thrall to the thrill of petty dramas and victimhood; to believe they are in danger or persecuted by others is justification enough for their self-indulgent impulses and manipulations. But what you sow, so shall ye reap.

SOMETHING EXQUISITE THIS WAY COMES

To encounter beauty is to engage a living archetypal force; the ordinary mind and body have little resistance to its spiritual power–whether it be a landscape, painting or living person.

How often do you wonder through a beautiful park and encounter loud, vexatious, or disorderly people? Conversely, when you walk down a dank and tired old street, what do you notice about the people–their facial expressions, attire and demeanour? Each location has its own energetic orbit and point of attraction; beauty uplifts and inspires while its absence allows denser, more morbid energies to manifest.

During my teens I spent a weekend with some friends at a farmhouse on an island served by the Gulf Stream. We arrived in the evening by boat and went straight out to the pub. By the time we got to the house, on top of a hill overlooking the bay, it was pitch black. I lit a fire in my room and then drifted off into a drunken slumber. At first light, I awoke with a crushing headache; the smoke from the hearth had filled the room during the night and the copious amounts of alcohol in my system had left me dehydrated and quesy. I desperately hoped there would be a pharmacy in town offering some cure.

As I opened the creaky door, I was met by a vivid blue sky and sub-tropical warmth. Across the bay the hills glowed with purple heather and lush palm trees–much like the oversaturated colours on those old postcards. The sea lapped the shore and glittered in the sun. The effect was instantaneous; my head cleared and my body felt lighter. They say nature knows best, and she even brought her cure to my door.

During my final year at university I sought out part-time work to help pay the bills. Instead of being cooked up in a noisy, smokey pub, I opted for the outdoor adventures offered by the UK's Reserve Forces. On the first day of selection with the Royal Marines, we were shown into a room filled with military garb and told to find boots and clothes that fitted. As I was trying on a pair of boots, a voice behind me said: "I think you've got an odd pair there, mate." I turned around and was nearly knocked off my feet by the stunning face of this sub-lieutenant. The configuration of his features sent out a burst of ecstasy. I tried to compose myself and maintain my masculine composure–this was the marines after all–but spent the rest of the day trying to reconcile this new paradigm of the material world. The rigours of the selection process were henceforth much less real than this glimpse of purity in human form–though to others it would have remained merely a handsome face. For those accustomed to ugliness, it must come as a shock to encounter a physical manifestation of the sublime–how else to explain a property developer's ability to bulldoze a pristine woodland?

Some years later, after having reluctantly joined the world of work, I was strolling down the corridor in the office and gazed up at a woman coming towards me; once again her beautiful face triggered a blissed-out, incredulous state. Some weeks later, I was at my desk as someone glided over to the empty seat beside mine. A voice muttered: "When will he be back?" pointing at the vacant space. I glanced up and it was her; my jaw went into lockdown and my body became paralysed. I could only grunt through clenched teeth. She must have thought me a right oddball.

As with the previous encounter, this was no primordial lechery; it was an elevation of the consciousness, where the body was rendered redundant. Beauty's gaze was all consuming.

I can only think that the facial features of these two people carried some encryption–a sacred geometry of scale and composition–that triggered a response in the hidden depths of my being. The physical sensation in both cases was like receiving an internal massage while being injected with a strong opiate. To enter such a state is to feel vulnerable but receptive; it provides an invigorating release from the imperatives of the ego and body.

Much has been said about the hidden geometric structures incorporated in some of the world's great artistic masterpieces–most famously Michelangelo's *Mona Lisa*. Did these master painters and initiates of the secret societies hope to lower our guard by harnessing the attributes of beauty, before implanting some latent geometric template into our subconscious? Perhaps that explains Lisa's enigmatic smile: "There's more to me than meets the eye," she hints.

"By their fruits ye shall know them." Matthew 7:20

The brotherhood of Freemasons lead the colonisation of the New World, bringing with them the crude mechanics of empire and commerce. The native American tribes, long entrusted guardians of nature's virtue and equilibrium, were swept aside by the ambitious land-grab. Instead of integrating their host's organic wisdom with the efficiencies of production these self-appointed crusaders set about implanting their own grid-like structures on top of the existing natural "power points"[15]. What interest could they have in such esoterica, you may ask. Even a cursory examination of the positioning, the symbolism, the interrelated connections of the buildings erected by America's "founding fathers" betrays a hidden agenda–one handed down for generations and gleaned through exposure to more subtle realms.

Freemasons inherited template mechanics from their forefathers–the Templar knights (Templar = template). It would no longer be just portraiture and church vestibules that bore their geometric imprint; a whole continental landmass would become their new canvass. The lack of humility when faced with such a gift of Nature is both defining and symptomatic of their creed. It seems interesting that both the Anglo-Saxon Protestant power elite and their Catholic counterparts in Rome, though historically ideological enemies,[16] both borrow

---

15 Gridlines across the globe intersecting at regular points, otherwise known as Planetary Energetic Grid Theory, derived from Plato's hypothesis on platonic solids.

16 The Poor Fellow-Soldiers of Christ and of the Temple of Solomon, commonly known as the Knights Templar, the Order of the Temple or simply as Templars, were among the most wealthy and powerful of the Western Christian military orders and were among the most prominent actors of the Christian finance. The organisation existed for nearly two centuries during the Middle Ages.

Officially endorsed by the Catholic Church around 1129, the Order became a favoured charity throughout Christendom and grew rapidly in membership and power. Templar knights, in their distinctive white mantles with a red cross, were among the most skilled fighting units of

and utilise the symbolism and structural forms of ancient Egypt–the imported needle monolith; the peacock; pine (or pineal) cone; the great eye (of Horus); the classical pillars.

What would symbols of an ancient foreign culture be doing scattered about the Vatican or indeed in Washington, London or Paris? Unless, of course, they have some hidden significance that suggests a homage to a so-called barbarian epoch. The curved domes of the Sistine chapel, St Paul's Cathedral and that on Capitol Hill appear remarkably similar. Do they embody some esoteric power–as divine amplifiers, or perhaps giant symbols of the pineal gland (the psychic third eye)?

Though George Washington may be depicted ascending to the heavens on the inside of the US Capitol dome, the apotheosis of his contemporaries is less assured.

Somewhere along the line, the high ideals of these crusading knights were lost–or set aside. Geometric templates are not the only source of influence. The human consciousness and body are conduits of intention. To

---

the Crusades. Non-combatant members of the Order managed a large economic infrastructure throughout Christendom, innovating financial techniques that were an early form of banking, and building fortifications across Europe and the Holy Land.

The Templars' existence was tied closely to the Crusades; when the Holy Land was lost, support for the Order faded. Rumours about the Templars' secret initiation ceremony created mistrust and King Philip IV of France, deeply in debt to the Order, took advantage of the situation. In 1307, many of the Order's members in France were arrested, tortured into giving false confessions, and then burned at the stake. Under pressure from King Philip, Pope Clement V disbanded the Order in 1312. The abrupt disappearance of a major part of the European infrastructure gave rise to speculation and legends, which have kept the "Templar" name alive into the modern day. (Wikipedia)

scupper best laid plans, all you need is an agent of change. In chemistry it is called a dispersant and in group dynamics it is known as an infiltrator; both terms come into play in the more subtle realms of frequency. Like a cat among the pigeons, a dynamic group will often attract attention from those who covet its gains but reject its ethics. By guile or force the anomalous consciousness burrows in and wreaks havoc from within. It has to be said that the "dark" cabals of this world are also subject to such interventions. And so the game has continued down through the eons.

There is another manifest commonality between these elites–the course and nature of societies under their influence. Far from a utopian metropolis channeled from the heavens, we find suppression of ethnic natives, policies of foreign intervention, a system of financial hegemony and corporate-political statehood.

We are inclined to imbue others with our own attributes; as our perceptual filters often remain invisible and unexamined. So it is with some members of the power elite; they perceive the workings of a great mind in the cosmos–an overarching architect of life who formulated natural laws–but they feel abandoned to their own devices in a hostile world. The "deists" attempt to harness these laws to elevate themselves to the status of gods–with dominion their ultimate goal. They alone are qualified to fill the shoes of their absent and neglectful "father", or so they tell themselves. The movement from group identification towards elitism is fuelled by the differentiating characteristics of intellect and refined sensory acuity. The hidden manipulators of this material world were once part of the social miasma, where the more vulgar and hypocritical elements of the human condition began to impinge on their sense of welfare.

Instead of reconciling these irritations with a broader view of life, they sought out mechanisms to escape it, and later to decimate it.

This desire among certain groups to dominate and control has not lessened, but has proliferated and diversified. As civil liberties evaporate under the stifling onslaught of technological surveillance and "security" restrictions, many of us still seem unsure of who to trust and what to believe. We are told that religious fundamentalists pose a constant threat of attack while new epidemics arise each year that could wipe out whole sections of society. The same soothsayers are quick to offer prescriptive solutions; the corporate-political state implores us to give more powers to the police, to allow monitoring of more facets of our lives and to inject ever more cocktails of chemicals and bacteria to ensure our safety–the antidote to a toxin is to take another toxin, they assure us. Like children subject to an overbearing parent, we feel helpless and frustrated. These underlying antagonisms and hypocrisies erupt in the form of social strife or disease of the body, but still we make do with the soothing platitudes of politics and consumerism.

A recent survey of Georgians suggested that 43 per cent of them would like to have Stalin back; I know an eminent scientist who professes admiration for Hitler; the neo-conservatives in the US win over working class voters through the fear-mongering of patriotism, nationalism and tribalism–and yet Republican administrations progressively disenfranchise those very people through pro-corporation and anti-union policies. It's brilliant strategising, but is by now a well worn trick.

Platitudes can seem as a warming balm to the numbness of ignorance. A cognitive dissonance can ease the passage of hostilities, especially when whole nations are implicated. As the revolutions and purges of the past remind us, fundamental change can be traumatic. Better the devil you know, we say. But consider the forces behind most of the sudden societal collapses of the modern age; small groups with one objective–dominion and control. The ideological motifs of equality and emancipation that are used to rouse support are quickly discarded once their position has been consolidated. It takes a self-composed and self-aware individual to discern the wolf in sheep's clothing.

The wilful, self-assured individual can be quite beguiling–especially when they say there is work to be done and the enemy is at the door–after all they are offering to make the hard decisions on our behalf. Some people still cling to the memory of psychotic despots because at least they offered clearcut answers and removed the burden of personal responsibility. While there are people willing to hand over their power, there will be others only too glad to take it.

Chaos is the tool of the suppressor; better the gradual shaping influence of the elevated consciousness–with the collective consciousness of society informed enough to take or leave it.

Esotericists pandering rationality? Why? Because the rational mind is designed for day-today processes–getting from a to b; engaging with the material world around you. The rational mind is a perceptual box; if you are in a box, then you are contained, restricted; you are easily moved around.

Many people seem unable to countenance the idea that institutions ostensibly set up to serve them could be progenitors of disharmony and strife, but they fail to examine the personality issues underlying such groups or organisations. What is the motivation of someone who wants to have "power", to be in charge? Where are their mental processes situated–the primal reptilian centres of the brain or something more sophisticated? What is their propensity to be "corrupted"; to enter a silo mentality; to adopt a "them and us" perspective? Were all of the teachers you had at school really suited to nurturing the minds of a new generation of humans? It wasn't all that long ago that head masters were dispensing the corporeal punishment to "wayward" pupils.

We are to some extent defined by the questions you ask–for the answers are almost always forthcoming–therefore if you are happy to be spoon-fed wholesale answers to questions you haven't asked, then don't be surprised if the results are a bit bewildering.

They might have your mind and body, but they can't take your Soul.

Sensitivity–much maligned and often confused with emotionality–is your inbuilt mobile phone, navigation system, divining rod, portable computer and personal adviser rolled into one. It is also your greatest inheritance, because it provides the key to ultimate freedom. I could be having a conversation with someone in the office or over the phone and I start to see and feel the underlying characters and factors in their point of focus. They might be discussing a relative having had a baby–in which case I might see its gender and name–or about a long-lost uncle they would like to see again–where I might see his face and location. Sometimes I throw in details that I couldn't have known about, according to rationality, and this may elicit surprise from my counterpart, but more often they keep on talking as if they didn't hear what I just said–presumably because it is an impossibility, therefore their mind cannot accept it even happened. After all, what can you expect from a man–a mere Cro-Magnon with modern designer clothes?

Men, more than women, have banished this "cosmic" inheritance from memory, probably because they have dutifully embraced the role as pragmatic hunter-gatherer. We all have these impulses of insight, but all too often dismiss them in favour of a conventional, mind-oriented answer. But once you accept that you are a living antenna for other people's thoughts and actions–past, present and future–you begin to discern the subtle difference in the signals. The Self sometimes deals in abstractions or will highlight salient generalities, as it delivers you the essence of the situation–and it is this essence that transcends outward machinations or appearances and which constitutes the bigger Truth. More importantly you begin to cultivate a relationship with the larger intelligence that is you. Its counsel can be initially perplexing but, given the benefit of hindsight or a satisfying conclusion to events, it eventually becomes a trusted source. The realisation that you–the mere reflection of that grander Self–are never alone establishes a comfortable platform on which to better sculpt your life, with less self-doubt and less neurosis. The gratitude and humility engendered by this relationship is also empowering in itself–both of these states are akin to opening your arms to the cosmos, which is inclined to hug you back.

Ask and ye shall receive, goes the immortal promise–but ask a flippant question and you get a flippant answer.

Mean what you say and say what you mean–then allow yourself a dignified, mature response.

The Self is always gentile and illuminating, never dogmatic or insistent. Where it resides there is no hurry or panic. As you identify more with its nature and come to realise its attributes in yourself, you move closer to the mind of God–in a gradual process of refinement and alignment.

Once you begin to identify with something that is in many ways outside your little self, you start to realise that the other little identities out there, as it were, are equally valid and worthy. The tags and monikers you have picked up on your journey–shy, timid, handsome, ugly, cantankerous, mean, clumsy, academic, sporty or whatever–hold less sway as you view them as largely narrow, incomplete projections of others. By rising above these assumptions, you gain the scope to cast them off. The stored traumas and guilts fade in power as the situations that generated them are revealed as plot points in a microscopic play. The mechanisms of the illusory world become more apparent–intuition peers beyond the surface detail at the underlying intention that generated the situation in the first place. You may not be able to see all the "causes" of the current "effects" but you begin to appreciate the relationship: a thought becomes a desire, which then becomes manifest. The energy originated with you, so it will seek to return to you. Ralph Waldo Emerson's maxim comes to life: "… what you are shouts so loudly in my ears"–be it an individual, government or whole civilisation.

People sometimes exclaim in surprise: "How do you know that?!" If I were to put discretion aside, I would reply: "How can I not know it?"

And what is there to know? Well, everything and anything.

As you become more transparent and less prejudiced, so others of a similar persuasion move into your orbit. It is gratifying to be viewed by someone with fewer perceptual filters and more insight; you are no longer an unknown quantity waiting to be tagged and bagged. Your relationships have a chance of becoming organic and developmental, rather than preconceived conventions borrowed from popular culture or academia.

THINGS CAN ONLY GET BETTER

A nephew of my father's was asked to babysit for my two brothers and I one Saturday when we were still of primary school age. It was suggested he take us for lunch and then to the cinema. He accepted the latter, but not the former–pocketing the cash, no doubt. It was perhaps ironic that this self-confessed laggard took us to see *Superman*. On leaving the performance my state of mind was transformed; I was no longer the vulnerable, timid nine-year-old but something invincible and unrestricted. If I hadn't had the responsibility of my siblings, I would have flown off there and then! Every molecule of my being had been infused with some great archetypal Truth–at last, a glimpse of man's true nature; Kal-El's laser vision had blasted away the myopia of the masses.

This wonderful narrative not only delivered a box-office smash but has endured in the collective mind ever since. What at first glance is a ridiculous premise–a man in a cape from a distant planet defying the rules of gravity–eludes to a quandary that gets scant debate in "serious" intellectual circles; the prospect that this island Earth is not the cutting edge of evolution in the universe. Perhaps the fascination with the Superman story–indeed, the "S" actually being a heraldic designation representative of "hope" on Krypton–is derived from its precognition of where humanity is headed. If we briefly entertain the notion that linear time is but a construct designed to give a limited consciousness the notion of moving from A to B or that this "cause" will equal this "effect", then we open to the possibility that the past, present and future are simultaneous. Superman's real power lies in his ability to connect audiences to that very real, present future. As I walked down the street afterwards, the veil between the present and the future me had peeled back; I had dipped my toe into that empowered state of consciousness.

Superman has free reign and limitless dominion over all of humanity, should he desire it–but he doesn't desire that; his consciousness is posited in a realm of greater truth that renders any such ambitions futile and counter-productive. He forsakes much of his invisibility to reach out and engage with Earth's civilisation, so that it might also ascend to a more lofty status (one where self-servers and the power-hungry could not exist by virtue of their intentions and limited perceptual scope). The highly material self-image of the "self-centered" individual is just that; flesh and blood desiring physical comforts and sensations. That perspective is both defined by and limited to that gross existence, mistaking form as the only function. When someone said, "the meek shall inherit the Earth", I suspect they meant that the "meek" would remain tied to that limited physical space, while others took on a more cosmic, expanded existence. Those so-called rationalists who say, "I will only accept what I can explain logically" limit themselves to the parameters of their meek mental function; the brain is merely a translation tool, not the library itself. The mind (consciousness) begets matter, not the other way about.

Similarly, the enduring appeal of the James Bond character may not be that he effortlessly beds glamorous women or gets to drive elegant cars, but that his dynamism–a death-defying ability to usurp all evil and obstruction–is prototypical of the self-realised individual.

Superman's skin-tight blue uniform may not be so much a fashion statement as a suggestion that the human form takes on a different hue depending on its atmospheric or environmental settings. Would it be so strange to suppose that a human race would exhibit blue skin if that was a biological imperative on their host planet? It might also be assumed that, having developed the ability to fly, or levitate, a race of humanoids would routinely choose that method over walking, thereby affecting their physical evolution over time; they might have large heads and large eyes, with a body that tapers off in a streamlined fashion. At a deeper level, Superman may offer us an initiation of sorts into the reality of meeting extraterrestrial beings–not ugly, acquisitive monsters but more evolved and egalitarian races. Any serious discourse on the subject is barred, first by so-called scientists who say we cannot see any inhabitable planets through our telescopes, and second by the media, which casts the subject in terms of mad conspiracy theory or light-hearted hokum. Indeed, while working as a journalist, I was once asked to cover a "UFO" conference for the weekend magazine of a national broadsheet. I flew off to the event half expecting to find people talking in abstraction about lights in the sky or metallic disks whizzing past their windows. Instead, I discovered a community of academics, former astronauts, investigative journalists and political activists who presented compelling and hitherto unseen data and "evidence" of ET interactions with Earth. When I filed my article back at the newspaper, I was met with a stony silence; it evidently presented too credible a picture for them to accept. What would the advertisers say about this, they must have asked.[17] The article was, as we say in the business, spiked.

With such a prevalent attitude in the corridors of power, it is no wonder society as a whole barely considers such a scenario.

Science fiction writers have gone some way to surmise on the possibilities of intergalactic communities, though they all too often portray "cosmic" humans in the limited terms of their own consciousness–somewhat immature and restrained by quantum mechanics. The great leap in human development will always be consciousness-led; without it the mind will be left fumbling with endless equations and the primordial ego left to sabotage any breakthrough that might imperil its dominance. So, it might be safer for us to restrict our visible representations of ETs to that offered by the cinema. I once read a report of a "contactee" who claimed that the main difficulty faced by off-world visitors was that Earth humans had a "psychic stench".

"Psychic" and "cinema", now there's a toxic relationship. From *The Shining* to *Carrie* to *Scanners,* how well film studios have vilified the notion of extra-sensory perception and psychic power–for that is what it is, the power to cut through the "rational" orthodoxy and the bonds of dogma. The implied message is thus: "only a neurotic, unstable person could manifest these abilities, and look at all the trouble they cause! Don't even go there, it's the path to destruction!" What a tremendous lie.

____

17 See Appendix: Blue-sky Thinking

It might be true that there have been many conjurers throughout history who have sought self-gain by employing mind games and esoteric tricks, but deeper Truths and the dynamic laws of the cosmos are defined and organised by a mind that ultimately preserves the sanctity of life. To enter with those elemental forces through the guidance of the Soul guarantees an audience with the real "adults", and grownups don't mock their own children. This might seem like a divergence into abstraction, but sometimes it takes the figurative approach to keep you in the ball park.

The apparent hazard for those people realising the magnetic potential of their thoughts and desires is that a selfish desire begets a selfish response. How many times have I desired an object or outcome on a whim, only to receive it in the form I had imagined. But how often the prize has turned out to be devoid of substance and often with a sting in its tail; it brought more problems than it was worth. Instead of seeking the calming respite of my instinctual Self, I had reached out with desires manufactured by someone else, be it a consumer staple or societal "right of passage".

During one brief interlude, I began experimenting with traffic lights; I would seek to change them at will. The same little experiment would take place while I was sitting in the steam room at my local gym; I would choose a light and turn it off with my mind. Soon after opening this bag of tricks, I came across a parable about a young initiate of a monastic order who would disperse the rain clouds whenever he ventured out for a stroll. One day, as he was dosing under a tree, the master of his order approached and began kicking him with some severity. The youth jumped up in terror and exclaimed: "Master, what are you doing? Why do you strike me?"

to which the guru replied: "Look around you, do you see those fields over there? Look at the withered crops. What will the people eat if they cannot cultivate food in those parched fields?" The initiate realised the folly of his ways, and so did I. By all means sculpt your reality and dreams with pragmatic and imaginative force but try to remain deferential to the overarching interconnectedness of all life.

Indeed, a strong will can be felt immediately and tangibly. After leaving a conference with two associates, I offered a lift home to the one who lived near me; her friend, who was standing behind me, objected with such force that I felt a pulse of energy bounce off my back. She then vocalised her opinion with a curt: "No!"–ie. you WILL NOT take her and leave me.

As I headed for the exit one night after a particularly hectic day at the office, the cumbersome, antiquated revolving door loomed as usual. It was so heavy to push that I would invariably bang into me from behind as it caught up with me before I escaped out the other side. On this night, however, it just moved as I approached; in fact it moved so perfectly in time with my pace that I did not need to slow down or even lift a finger; I breezed through like it didn't exist. On reaching the fresh air I silently congratulated the management for automating the old door. The next day the door was back to its old self. I made a joke to the security guards about the one-day technological marvel, but instead of a laugh got a perplexed look. "What do you mean, James?" said the head of security. I told him how well it had worked the night before, but he shook his head: "The door was never automated. In fact, it will be replaced soon."

Another anomalous incident to consign to the miscellaneous section of my memory banks. And so it might have remained–had I not enquired to myself as I approached the entrance some months hence: "Who or what did that?" There was a man and woman standing outside smoking and chatting; as I came within earshot, the man's subdued chatter suddenly rose on the words: "He was an angel."

Not only was the door opened unto me but the answer was immediately forthcoming on asking. The most abiding effect of such experiences is not that one is afforded a glimpse of the paranormal but that the humility and gratitude engendered by it can only bring you closer to God.

The mysterious realm of angels has become the New Age movement's alternative hunting ground for answers as the dubious counsel of conventional clairvoyants–purportedly communing with deceased human relatives–renders itself obsolete amid consistent deceit in matters of a predictive nature. For those seeking merely evidence of life after death, then the talented clairvoyant can provide a stunning evidential package; but it is when they are relied upon to make pronouncements about where and when you are going that the ruse–though almost never knowingly instigated–begins to take shape. Notwithstanding, these are mainly sincere and intuitive people, not the tricksters they are sometimes mistaken as.

The shape and hue of our current lives are the product of our many decisions taken since becoming conscious beings. That means we are all ultimately responsible for where we are at any given time, though there are many institutions and individuals who seek to influence our thinking. So, to hand over that innate freedom of choice to other, unseen forces just because they have impressed you with their ability to know details of your past and present–facts that could only be derived from paranormal intelligence–is nonetheless a negation of your own sovereign instinctual mechanism.

It has been proposed by some that childhood trauma can cause a fracture in the psyche into which spirits can enter haphazardly. A person may use magic in an immature or selfish way to initiate contact with outside forces and thereby lay a framework that lacks the authenticity of high ideals and principles. Without a degree of self-awareness or self-control, what chance does anyone have of conducting an orchestra of invisible players? These talented individuals often blindly trust the unseen voices or apparitions that come to them out of a self-effacing deference. But this is no place for the deluded or timid. The tried and trusted morale framework of the established initiation process–overseen and directed by masters of the art–was designed to avoid these pitfalls. Our consumer society has conditioned us to expect everything to come fast and easy–but you get what you pay for.

In my experience, it is not what is said but what is felt that determines the authenticity of any interaction–and that means it is you who remain the arbiter of your experience. Advice can be good; neglected facets of our lives can be highlighted; ill-judged actions reassessed, but the ruse–if it exists–comes when an individual develops a dependency on these non-physical interlocutors and makes decisions about their life based on these directions. Anybody who has been to see a clairvoyant knows that the residual "what ifs" or regrets about unrealised prophecies linger long after, like dark clouds.

The overt and formal structures of the New Age movement offer prescribed means of pursuing "spiritual"
goals. It would seem the transformative techniques of
the ancient Mystery Schools are now accessible to all.
It only takes a workshop or two to gain a qualification
in this or that discipline–be it angel reader, reiki master,
crystal healer or channeler. Therefore it would seem that
the distance between the student and the teacher these
days is very short. The common ground is the acceptance of the given discourse on offer. This might impart
a more egalitarian tone to proceedings, but in some
cases amounts to the blind leading the blind.

A theoretical determinism can often overshadow proceedings. A common refrain from a fellow workshop
participant might be: "What star sign are you?"

"...Ah, well you are like that then, aren't you?" Or, "I
am a generous person and have connections to Archan-
gel Michael." Or, "Well, this book I'm reading says that
you can only ascend if you do these techniques."

The tone might be self-reverential but seems designed
only to convince the speaker of his or her own self-
worth and veracity. In other words, those who are really
convinced of their multi-faceted, multi-dimensional,
God-like status rarely feel driven to make public proc-
lamations. This is not a blanket dismissal of the process
for "enlightenment" offered by this modern social
strata, but merely a caution for those about to enter the
maze. The apparent disappointments and dead ends encountered while partaking in this faculty's cosmological
curriculum can be the greatest learning experiences in
the march towards graduation from the ego–if they direct you back to your inner Self.

Those people seeking answers outside of the more orthodox religions (and in doing so perhaps overlooking the portent and meaning contained in the scriptures) can end up just substituting one linguistic vernacular for another. To go through the motions is not enough; intention and consideration are the keys to embodiment. Just as Sunday Mass is used by some as a social excursion–an opportunity for neighbourly scopophilia or gossip–so the New Age forum serves the judgmental gaze of those determined to cast around the room looking to ascertain their "spiritual" status in the present hierarchy.

In the pursuit of spirituality or enlightenment, a person can read fervently, attend seminars, visit gurus and pay a king's ransom for other paraphernalia, but how often they overlook one of the greatest spiritual teachers just under their nose–the young child. Its playfulness, transparency and capacity for unrestrained joy is shared with the most magnificent beings in the heavens. Unsettled by this discord between them and us, we take it upon ourselves to ply them with our untested and outdated values and "protectively" smother them in the dogma of vulnerability. The cushion and resilience found in young children is largely of their own design; they instinctively feel limitless and empowered, therefore, while that instinct prevails, they are just that. They revel in the power of their imaginations–no less real than the material blandishments that are proffered to them by "adults". Those on a spiritual path would be wise to show reverence and humility before young children along the way.

When my daughter was two years old, I took her to an open weekend at a private estate nearby–with its stately home, exotic trees and expansive lake. She immediately felt in her element and rushed off to explore this new landscape. On reaching the edge of the lake, she gazed out in wonder at the birdlife perusing its surface. Then, to her left, a giant black bird raised it head and unfolded its huge wings in preparation for flight. A series of loud cracks, echoed across the lake as this avian jumbo began its transition from water to air. My daughter stood entranced as this new paradigm unfolded before her eyes. The bird passed her close by and, in an act of gravity-defying strength, broke away from the water's hold. As it turned to face into the lake, it added a triumphant squawk to the rhythmic whip and crack of the colossal wings. My daughter, now directly facing its flight path, responded with a squeal of delight that addressed the whole lake, and raised her arms in sympathy with what she was seeing. The bystanders seemed both delighted and profoundly touched by the demonstration of self-expression and communion coming from this small child.

I recall watching a TV programme many years before, where so-called anthropologists and historians "explored" South American myths about giant condors swooping down and stealing the babies of tribe-folk. How consistently the mainstream media present this upside-down view of the natural world, where Man's technological conquest has nullified the inherent dangers of the wilderness. The condors may well have lifted babies into the air, but in an act of communion that introduced them to Nature's symbiotic and collaborative purpose for Mankind. The physiological thrill of being privy to such a display and/or of being elevated to look down from another perspective, I would propose, opens up levels of consciousness beyond the ego-self that can then connect with the Mind of Nature—thereby creating an invisible, yet stabilising, bond that will last that individual a lifetime; a true Motherly embrace. The next time you hear a horror story about the dangers of the wild, just flip it over and you will get closer to the truth.

J.R.R. Tolkein railed against industrialisation's demolition of the pastoral idle in *The Lord of the Rings* books. His orcs and wraiths sought to externalise their own inner desolation and grotesqueness throughout Middle Earth, while the elves and hobbits remained in communion and symbiosis with nature, to their mutual benefit. Not only did Tolkien elegantly render the archetypal forces at play in the world, but he foresaw the shape of events that would unfold into the present day. For those with "eyes" to see, the energetic profile of people can appear just as gnarled or sublime as his polarised characters.

There was a government road safety campaign on television when I was a child which featured David Prowse as the Green Cross Code Man. His mantra was: "Stop, Look, Listen." That maxim may save you from the perils of the urban jungle–but it also serves as instruction in the verdant jungle–where Mother Nature awaits you patiently.

Environmentalism may be society's doctrine for countering threats to nature but it too has become monolithic–fundamentalist in its fervour and assumptions, with a reluctance to adapt or integrate other premises.

There is an emerging movement built on the promise of "clean" technology; allegedly covered up by governments in collusion with the $300 trillion oil industry. Once again we see a scientific–or even metaphysical framework–that makes sense on paper and may well translate into working systems. Like the Templars and

Freemason's of old, there is an assumption that because it comes from "out there" somewhere and appears to have been happened upon, that it is a natural formulation. The esoteric community once sought to harness the power of ascendant beings–to bring heaven to Earth–but by seeking power outside of themselves, as those afflicted with inferiority complexes are inclined to do, they failed to question the motives and character of the "illumined" non-physical minds they engaged. Have the technological concepts emerging from the launchpad of the internet really had their symbiotic organic nature considered, or are these progenitors of the free-energy utopia falling into the same trap as those who came before them–by making the assumption that if it's new and shiny, then it must be good? Certainly, though, it is high time someone suggested an alternative to the crude propulsion mechanics of exploding hydrocarbons and metal grinding on metal. Our senses have been assailed by the combustion engine for nigh on a hundred years. What if our "machines" were composed of living organisms–responsive and self-repairing–where their use was based on a partnership with their driver? At one time, and for some people, the horse and rider was a symbiotic relationship that took companionship to levels not experienced even among other humans.

There are universal laws, but it seems laws are meant to be broken–until such time as their sanctity and perfection is fully realised by all. Until then, we will be left spinning on the karmic wheel, obliged to pay off our debts.

Do we assume that because a galaxy has a black hole at its centre–sucking in all light and matter–that this is an organic, naturally occurring phenomenon? Does not the Moon seem too large for a planet of this size? Indeed, is it even the same age as Earth? If our lunar satellite is indeed anomalous, then where did it come from and what interstellar machinations (and motivated intelligence) plopped it into this orbit? In a universe of ascending frequencies, what does the stasis imposed by its rhythmic ebb and flow (manifest in the tidal system) really mean for the planet's genesis?

On the other hand, could it be that this "anomalous" relationship between planet and satellite is what maintains the delicate ecological balance that allows material life to flourish here? In esoteric teachings, the Moon is the feminine influence to balance the masculine force of the Sun. An interesting geometry is revealed when the moon momentarily eclipses the sun; the distance between the three celestial bodies allows for the precise coverage of the star when viewed from Earth.

Because it is sitting there in the sky, we seem to just accept that it must have emerged in symbiosis with the planet. Science has in many cases managed to square the circle by force of will alone; quite an achievement. The small-minded insistence–against all available evidence–that the cosmos is a series of random events may maintain rational Man at the top of the tree, but it also robs him of his greatest inheritance–a visceral, immersive communion and ability to direct that very cosmos.

Imagine a mouse sitting on a shaft of wheat in a field way into the future. The farmer planted a genetically modified variant of the crop in the hope that it would be more resistant to pests. By this time mice have evolved a rudimentary understanding of chemistry and biology; they gaze out at the universe of the wheat field and behold its genetic structure, assuming in the process that this is a naturally occurring, organic system. One day the mouse hitches a ride on a passing hawk and is taken beyond the border of its vast domain and into a wheat field cultivated without genetic modification. There it discovers a universe of more diverse life, and on inspecting the surrounding molecular structure it finds a rather different proposition. It does not yet perceive the mechanism of the intelligence behind the wheat and has not yet taken the next step of deducing that man has manipulated the previous structure with ulterior motives–this is as yet too much of a leap of consciousness for a species that has just gotten over the shock of inter-field travel.

My point is that the sheer weight of physical mass and scope of geological timeframes have an uncanny ability to subdue the questioning mind of our little selves. How many times at school did I stay silent in class to preserve the status quo, instead of interrogating the teacher over her staid pronouncements on this or that subject. On the rare occasions that I did, it felt like the piano had stopped playing in the Wild West saloon.

I once went to buy some bric-a-brac at a hardware store in rural Spain. I was introduced to the owner–a woman beyond retirement age–as "James from England". My native companion briefly left me behind while she went to change some euro notes next door. While waiting I asked a few simple questions in lucid Spanish, but all the woman could say was: "No entiendo, no entiendo," while shaking her hand. She simply refused to believe that she could understand anyone from another country.

Another native of that country spoke excellent English when I first met him in London, but on the next occasion–in Madrid–he could barely form a sentence. It would be a fair assumption that the expectations engendered by the differing environments accounted for the disparity.

It will require a critical mass of people to consistently question the evidence under their own noses (or, in some cases, just beyond them) to sweep away old, unchallenged assumptions.

POLITICAL INCORRECTNESS

My first job was in advertising–as a graphic artist. I left the industry many years ago but the idiom lives on. Most of our interactions seem to be couched as commercial propositions. Advertising speak pervades social discourse; the collective mind has adopted commercial values for many facets of life–from relationships to the prestige of a job. We define ourselves by the brand of car we drive, the clothes we wear or even the cosmetics that adorn our skin.

It's true that you can gauge a person's values by their grooming and attire–if that is their method for making a personal statement–but what about those people who aren't so eager to identify with superficial categories? Well, you might try looking into their eyes.

To share the aims or values of a group is indeed a comfort. How else are we "socialised" or initiated into the orthodoxy. The school pupils who have an aptitude for passing exams are told they are the brightest–in the terms one might describe the efficiency of a computer. Those with the highest marks are courted by institutions of the state–the sciences, the law, the media. They will have worked hard to become part of that elite, and will not easily question the received wisdom offered therein, as to do so would be a direct challenge to their identity. Their self-esteem has been built on, dare I say, such banalities and therefore risks deconstruction. Indeed, look at the fruits of their labour—a nice house, a big car, and eventually a title or two.

Many of us are afraid of new paradigms—we moan about the mundane course of our lives or about what other people are doing to the world, and yet we will pounce on anyone who proffers to challenge the status quo. To consider the fundamentals of existence in a new light is not to undermine the hard-fought construct that is you, but is an opportunity to expand—to become something larger and more connected.

By being open to new ideas, you not only allow more scope for identity but align yourself with others who are also prepared to launch personal missions of discovery. We are individually and collectively defined by the questions we ask. If we shun all queries we become more subject to the world of artifice and commercially derived pastiche. It might be stating the obvious, but time spent "alone" can be a great facilitator of self-awareness; we begin to separate from the caricature imposed on us by others and start to feel the underlying motives and uniqueness of our self. With this periodic cleansing we can refresh ourselves more authentically from within and without.

To be reduced to a series of predictable habits for the convenience of others is to be regarded no more regally than by an advertiser trying to sell you something; social or economic categorisation amounts to much the same thing. Take the biological self—even a cursory appraisal of a book on anatomy will reveal the mechanisms of a magnificent, adaptive, dynamic vessel. Then consider the human consciousness that gave form to it as even more multifaceted and ingenious.

As a foolhardy youngster, I sought the chemical relief of cigarettes. It was only after having a series of profound "dreams", where its effects on my body were spelt out, that my motivation shifted–and I quickly quit the weed. This counsel by the Self is more prescient and benevolent than any commercial on TV. To even begin to acknowledge its existence is to embark on the journey of the adept and master–both of which are you. The self-destructive urges of the smoker dissipate under the reverential regard of the inner voice. The dialogue between the self and the Self surpasses all platitudes.

OH, NOT THAT AGAIN

My final-year thesis at university was on propaganda. I started reading *Mein Kampf*[18] to gain an insight into the motivations of its author, but gave up after a few pages. The self-reverential tone and limited scope of the treatise betrayed the mind of an immature, paranoid and, of course, wilful being. This level of consciousness was all too familiar; it was as apparent in the school bully as it was in a ruthless company director. Those who identify with this perspective are easily induced into its evidence-based reality–they frequently encounter people they consider to be stupid or deceitful, but they fail to grasp their own part in this nightmare, as the director. You get what you focus on.

We often refer to such people as "animals". But animals are loyal subjects of their collective mind; their guiding force. The maniacal ego mind inhabits a world of inner chaos and self doubt and seeks respite by transferring that disharmony to the world around it. In the hierarchy of life, this brazen archetypal force resides at the weighty end of subjective existence–burdened by a focus on the crudest matter.

18 The autobiographical manifesto of Nazi leader Adolf Hitler, published in 1925.

On arriving in Montreal in the late 70s, we moved into a rented apartment in the Westmount suburb. The block of flats had a resident janitor from the Ukraine who had a Colombian wife and two children. It wasn't long until my siblings and I were acquainted with the boy and girl of a similar age; and it was not long after that that the mother started making accusations about the theft of their toys. Her energy was something new to me, and even for an eight-year-old it was palpably disturbing. Things escalated somewhat and my sister became the focus of her ire. One day my mother took us to the local outdoor pool where the Colombian woman and her children were also in attendance. My sister was paddling water in the busy pool, when suddenly something pulled her under. She gasped for breath, but a determined hand held her down. In a last desperate effort she reached out and made contact with the face of her attacker; she kicked free and made for the side of the pool. The janitor's wife had sought to unleash her pathological hatred in an act of murder.

Many years later I would be introduced to the mother of a prospective girlfriend; on meeting her eyes, the Colombian woman was there staring back through the depths of time–the same archetypal force was once again making its presence felt; the same combination of distrust and simmering anger; a will to dominate and control. I should have run for the door there and then. It begs the question, why did that familiar "foe" return to my experience? What had I not learnt from the last encounter–or, rather, what had I not let go?

A PROBLEM SHARED

Feminism is but a reactionary movement–a fight fire with fire approach. It is hardly a reinterpretation of what it means to be a woman or an advanced discourse for society; it says, if you can't beat them, join them. Some of the most aggressive, dogmatic people I have encountered were self-professed feminists. The timely and noble aspirations of the suffragettes have been hijacked by people with personal agendas–and emotional baggage. The early social and political gains seem to have been offset by the hypocrisy of its proponents, who embody the very behaviour they condemn. So-called feminist literature my be a useful forum for women to realise shared experiences but why must it be so conditional and categorised–as if to say, if you find common ground here then you should fully embrace our plan of action or adopt our mindset? Indeed "feminist" writing is just as pertinent to men, as it is a mirror on the silo mentalities that exist in patriarchal fraternities. Ultimately, though, it seems many women have merely swapped one prison cell for another–social confinement for spiritual confinement. The simmering resentment at having to behave like a man to get on in the world is as much a consequence of betraying their natural tendencies as it is a frustration with men per se. At the end of the day, everybody has the choice to be themselves.

The enigmatic power and foresight possessed by the female oracles and maternal fraternities of old must have deeply antagonised the supercilious male ego. It is no surprise then that the feminine attributes have been maligned and suppressed, but these past custodians of wisdom derived their poise and fortitude from their connection to the Divine Mother–or aspects thereof–not from the connivance of their own egos.

If those male protagonists could have only realised that Her secrets were available to them too–if only they could learn to let go, trust, and embrace that which repulsed them, as any great Mother would do. The Great Womb offers succour to all–and therein lies its power.

A life of balance is one where both men and women blend, so to speak, harmoniously with each other and their surroundings. For too long men have felt obliged to fulfil a narrow, masculine role and women have been confined to more placid "nurturing" roles–both blanket impositions that are designed to facilitate a homogenous workforce, and which commonly generates frustration and anger. We humans–whatever our outward gender–are blends of the feminine and masculine. It is only we, the individuals, who can discern what mixture of both makes us feel empowered and complete. It is a journey of discovery that is all too often sidelined by the superficial blandishments or impositions of a industrial society. The journey needn't be a selfish negation of responsibilities to find oneself, but can be the road to greater self-acceptance, and therefore more acceptance and compassion for others.

The trials and tribulations people put themselves through in the game of the sexes almost defies logic; we subject ourselves to judgmentalism and compromise our instincts to fit in with the perceived wisdom that only someone in a "relationship" is a credible personality. But how many people compromise themselves for the sake of convenience or social standing? Our identities are closely tied to this ritual starting during our school days; if you get to the end of your sojourn through the "education" system and haven't had a few girlfriends or boyfriends you feel a failure. For that reason alone it is often a relief to get out into the wider world where less scrutiny is focused on the individual's social affairs. And yet the habitual superficial gaze is no more rewarding than looking at a steak on a plate; the social meat market has much in common with the slaughter house.

For the more idealistic, the search for a Twin Flame of Soul Mate can be as elusive as it is undefined. But for the male who has acknowledged and integrated the feminine aspect of his self and the female who has embraced her dynamic masculine attributes, that search for unity is in many respects complete. The imbalance has been addressed and therefore the cravings dissipate. That said, the rounding of the individual personality is the priming required for a synergistic union with another–where the gaps have been filled in and the self-delusions exposed.

IF THE CAP FITS

As a child, I had memories of places and experiences–and, more particularly, of emotional bonds with other people–that obviously were not derived from my short existence in my short body. They were the perceptions of an adult–or at least not of a child. An ingratiating life in the middle ages, a searing exposure to warfare in the early 20th century, and many other disparate encounters, would flash up as anomalous fragments charged with emotion. They soon receded into the ether as the dullness of the current incarnation drained any inherent vitality.

The idea of reincarnation–and exploring past lives through hypnosis–has been embraced at times by the mainstream media, but it would take me 40 years to pursue that particular indulgence. My Amazon account had taken to recommending books by an American hypnotist, which I ignored, until one day stumbling across an interview with her online. She claimed to have developed a technique that could access the deep subconscious, or higher self, and she displayed a self-assuredness that was lacking from the TV hypnotists. So, in honour of those now almost forgotten dalliances from my childhood, I tracked down one of her contemporaries in London. In the hypnotic state, I "became" a man sitting in a huge cathedral-like building, draped in a red gown and sporting a domed hat. In fact, the transportation took place just before she prompted: "Go to a life that has some importance." The concurrent realisation was that this middle-aged man was a pope. A stream of questions revealed that he was based in France, at a palace-cum-cathedral that he had commissioned, and that he had also funded a large basilica or oratory (there or somewhere else) which was in fact an amplifier for communion with higher realms–or God, as he put it. This was his unspoken pact with the people of this country, in answer to their requests for help with their spiritual goals. There was widespread ignorance of this matter among the cardinals, who he perceived as egotistical and careerist.

The castellated, sandy-coloured palace seemed to rise from the dusty landscape that surrounded it. This was a parched land with little vegetation close by. My doubts about a French pope were pushed aside as the questions came thick and fast. Peering out from his bedroom, this man could feel the warmth of the people towards him; their trust in his benevolence; their desire to be of noble character. It was a naive rural innocence that was in thrall to a more sophisticated and yet selfish court system. His loyalties therefore seemed to remain with them, rather than with the institution of which he was head.

The king of this land visited the pope in his palace and asked for guidance about the prospect of war with England–something that the influential court was pushing for. The pope merely advised the king to remember the techniques (presumably meditative) that they had discussed and practised and suggested that he try and remain within that meditator's consciousness, lest he be pulled into the scheming of his fear-mongering courtesans. Judging by the agitated response from the king, this would not be so–though the pope remained impassive. The next question from the hypnotist led me to a square where three elegantly dressed men in their 30s were being executed. The pope–or rather I–watched from a distance and took in the emanations of honesty and decency of the three men. It appeared that they had become the scapegoats in some plan of the king's court– perhaps they had opposed the war with England. The gathered crowd knew nothing of the real reasons for their impending deaths but blindly trusted the mechanisms of their rulers–the prevalent consciousness among the people was once again of a fundamental decency but also of considerable naivety.

Perched on a hillside, this pope was viewing a long line of ornately decorated soldiers streaming past on the road below–the road to war. Once again he was sanguine in the knowledge that people must be allowed to experience their free will, and that this was just one more scenario in the long play involving human egos. He was reassured to know that the proximity of the soldiers to himself meant that they would maintain a level of composure and compassion in battle–that they would not be inclined to degenerate into their more basal, animal selves by virtue of their exposure to his "energy". Indeed, this would be the foundation of his seemingly unpragmatic stance in the face of such belligerence–that he affected events and behaviours benignly through his invisible emanations; the power, and purity, of his consciousness.

For a week afterwards I could feel the mind of this man in symbiosis with my own; it was both profound and humbling to have accessed this wonderful character from the past–my past it would seem.

I got hold of a list of popes–all 266 of them–with mug-shots in tow. Scrolling down the faces, I was drawn to one in particular: Benedict XII, otherwise known as Jacques Fournier. There seems to be little written about his life and papacy, though there were enough salient facts to raise hairs on the back of my neck. There is a listing on Wikipedia, which I include below.

Fournier succeeded Pope John XXII as Pope in 1334, being elected on the first ballot of the papal conclave. A common practice at the time was for Cardinals to vote for a Cardinal who was not considered a real possibility for the papacy on the first ballot, in order to see how the other Cardinals were leaning. However, this time, an unusual thing happened: every Cardinal except Cardinal Fournier independently voted for Fournier. The Cardinals had not planned this, so the accession of the obscure Fournier on the first ballot was an entirely accidental affair.

Benedict XII was a reforming pope who did not carry out the policies of his predecessor. He chose to make peace withHoly Roman Emperor Louis IV, and as far as possible came to terms with the Franciscans, who were then at odds with the Roman See. He tried to curb the luxuries of the monastic orders, though without much success. He also ordered the construction of the Palais des Papes in Avignon.

Benedict spent most of his time working on questions of theology. He rejected many of the ideas developed by John XXII. In this regard, he promulgated an apostolic constitution, Benedictus Deus, in 1336. This dogma defined the

Church's belief that the souls of the departed go to their eternal reward immediately after death, as opposed to remaining in a state of unconscious existence until the Last Judgment. Though some claim that he campaigned against the Immaculate Conception, this is far from clear. He engaged in long theological debates with other noted figures of the age, such as William of Ockham and Meister Eckhart.

Though born a Frenchman, Benedict felt no patriotism towards France or her king, Philip VI. From the start of his papacy, relations between him and Philip were frigid. After being informed of Philip's plan to invade Scotland, Benedict hinted that Edward III, King of England would most likely win, regardless.

From the dates of his papacy–1334 to 1342–it is obvious that he was three years into the job when the Hundred Years War kicked off, so the deliberations between the king of France and himself were indeed significant. Also, it was news to me that popes were once based in France, in this case Avignon, and wore red garments. His papacy ends at his death on April 25, 1342–the day and month of my birth date. What clinched it though was when I looked up a photograph of the Palais des Papes in Avignon–the same sandy coloured mix of castle and cathedral. Though it would no doubt have been embellished over the years, the fundamental shape and aspect is just as I saw it–with its high-ceilinged atrium and storied windows.

The Soul, in its reductionist, fragmented material form– i.e. inhabiting a body here on Earth–would seem to have a particular focus and objectives. Depending on its level of maturity, or experience, it may be following a curriculum of self-development, as opposed to a more devotional service to others–as would befit a more seasoned being. That journey may involve many incarnations on Earth or elsewhere and span many thousands of years in our timeframe. To glance into those other lives may provide insights into those larger goals, as common traits and scenarios are revealed to the–in this case hypnotised–subject. Though Jacques Fournier was of a different epoch and social milieu, his overall orientation and objectives find a reflection in my own life. Fournier's obesity later in life was caricatured by his enemies; while I was reminded routinely as a young adult about my thin frame. Extremes beget extremes; the pendulum will move from one polarity to the other if infused with enough energy–and in life that driving force can be behavioural or emotional. The old adage rings true: moderation in all things. It was said Benedict "inveighed vigorously against greed for gain among ecclesiastics... and displayed a zeal for doctrinal and moral reform",[19] a stance that could equally be applied to me as I observe the various institutions of state in the modern world.

Not only was the past brought into the present for examination, but the present was forthcoming in validating that past.

---

19 Catholic Encyclopedia, Robert Appleton Company, 1912

START AS WE MEAN TO GO ON

When René Descartes formulated his "common sense" approach to life–i.e. doubt everything that can be doubted and hope that what is left over is Truth–the emerging "scientific" community of the early 19th century picked up the ball and ran with it. We now find ourselves at a point where objective reality is that which can be proven through measurable instruments based on the five senses. Not only that, but the results of those experiments and investigations are filtered through individuals with certain agendas, and so the already narrow truths become half-truths and even overlooked truths, until we find ourselves in a place of contradictions and even great ignorance parading as knowledge. On the bright side–as there always is–this level of ignorance can be seen as the great test of the individual; as the institutional dogmas loosen their hold and the old certainties are fragmented by technology's material alienation, then we are faced with the inevitable reductionist ultimatum–Who am I?

There is one last abstraction that I would like to share with you–and I will refer to it as the "donut of light." Some years ago I set out to quantify and gain some validation for the more subtle processes of communing with the non-physical consciousnesses that surround us;

previously "they" had come to me; now I would do some legwork. I quickly came across a prominent "channeler" based in London who ran workshops throughout the year. It was fascinating to observe words and pictures being delivered seemingly from somewhere outside of the ego mind and on cue. The person I had been part-nered with for a particular exercise had enquired about the nature of reality; the answer, as it appeared to me, was simply a donut of light set amid the void. I could only describe what I was seeing, without being able to explain intellectually at the time.

The mythic hero's journey eludes to the Wheel of For-tune or the Wheel of Karma–a journey that returns to where it started. Joseph Campbell eruditely described the cyclical path of the "Monomyth" in *The Hero with a Thousand Faces*.

You hear people say sometimes of a person, he or she is an old soul. That soul may have come further along the curvature of the circle, heading inextricably backs towards it source, but those people observing that in-dividual's ascendant qualities are also on that track, otherwise how could they share the same space? Some souls–becoming consumed by greed and anger–will zig-zag along that tunnel, temporarily dislodging and colliding with others in the process, but they remain within the embrace of the circle, also ultimately heading for completion. God beholds Himself in motion, with Her static womb forming the centre point.

Not unlike a roundabout at the swing park, the sensa-tion of motion is thrilling, even though we are not really going anywhere.

Who says donuts are not good for you?

God is Truth. To earnestly seek God is to earnestly seek the Truth. But realising the Truth means first facing the truth about yourself, and that is what holds many people back–the initially painful and sometimes shocking veracity of self-awareness. But once you make a commitment to that process, and it gets under way, progress to a purer state is rapid. The path towards God is the path to becoming God.

God is apparent in the reversal. All that you see and feel are the elements of a great mind that configure manifest reality. You can do what you like with those given elements, but you can't change their essential nature–therefore you cannot really go wrong. Those elements will always provide a benefit to life–a silver lining, as it were–even if employed for the most selfish and deluded purpose. The process of maturity is being able to perceive the totality of that elemental construct–and by then you won't want to change anything. As was conveyed to me once amid my despair, "everything is all right".

FEATURE ARTICLE

Blue-sky thinking

By James Zul

On a hot summer weekend in Sitges, along the coast from Barcelona, sun worshippers bask on the beaches. Perched atop a hill overlooking the town known throughout Spain as a mecca for the gay community, the Melia hotel hosts another group of people with their attention focused on the skies–but with barely a tan in sight.

More than 1,200 people have converged on the upmarket resort to hear former astronauts and US air force pilots, scientists, investigative journalists and academics take part in some "blue-sky thinking". The European Exopolitics Summit is something of a milestone for a country that was for so long, under Franco's regime, a closed shop on new ideas and something of a satellite state.

Dr Michael Salla, a co-founder of the movement, defines exopolitics as "the study of the political actors, institutions and key processes associated with the UFO phenomenon and the political implications of an extraterrestrial presence on Earth".

This definition suggests a more comprehensive study than mere UFOlogy. According to Dr Salla, UFO investigators have a physics background and analyse empirical data using quantitative methods, while exopolitics scholars mainly come from social sciences backgrounds and employ qualitative methodologies.

With a number of governments–including France, Germany, Denmark, Ireland, Sweden, Canada, Russia and to some extent Britain–having recently opened up their "UFO" files, such a summit is timely.

Figures from Britain's Ministry of Defence show that UFO sightings have soared to a 10-year high. Recently there were two near-misses with police helicopters and UFOs and an incident where a UFO was thought to have collided with a wind turbine in Lincolnshire. Nick Pope, who investigated UFO reports at the MoD between 1991 and 1994, explains some of the rationale behind the recent release of information.

"The Ministry of Defence receives more Freedom of Information Act requests about UFOs than any other subject. To me that is an amazing statistic, given that the government has troops in Iraq and Afghanistan. So, the department was absolutely swamped with these requests. By law they had to respond within twenty working days, and yet some of these requests were taking one hundred and twenty days... The MoD decided that the way to clear the backlog was to release all the information and send all the files to the National Archives, and then they could say, 'it's not our problem anymore'."

Perhaps the most startling evidence put before the conference is that from retired command Sergeant Major Robert Dean, who served in US Intelligence Field Operations and was stationed at Supreme Headquarters Allied Powers Europe, the military arm of Nato. He claims his Cosmic Top Secret clearance gave him access to a 1964 Nato report called "An Assessment", which acknowledged and analysed the implications of an alien presence on Earth.

"The study concluded this: Is there a threat to Allied forces in Europe? Apparently not. They concluded that planet Earth and the human race had been under some kind of observation for hundreds, if not thousands, of years. They concluded in 1964 that there were at least four different groups coming here, surveying us, analysing us. They concluded that there didn't appear to be a military threat involved, because the repeated demonstrations of incredibly advanced technology demonstrated to us that if they had been hostile, there would have been nothing we could have done about it.

"The United States just celebrated the 40th anniversary of putting a man on the moon. We went through this hoopty-doo, patting ourselves on the back; didn't we do good, putting a man on the moon...Well, my government, Nasa proceeded to erase 40 rolls of film from the Apollo programme; the flight to the moon; the flight around the moon; the guys walking here and there. We are talking about several thousand individual frames that the so-called authorities determined that you did not have the right to see.

"Well, thanks to the fact that there were a few employees in Nasa, forty years ago... decent people, honest people... I have some film that they preserved."

His first slide triggers a barrage of flashes and applause from the crowd. A man rushes to the stage with his camera phone in an effort to better frame the black and white moonscape.

The photograph carries the reference "Foto NASA AS-12-50-7348". Roll 50, negative number 7,348 shows the curved lunar surface taken from the Apollo 12 orbiter. However, hovering above the surface is a large saucer-shaped object.

The next slide is tagged "Cigar-shaped image taken by Neil Armstrong". It is just that; a long, luminous shape, with the moon's surface in the background.

"While they were looking out of the window of their craft, this object flew by. Neil took out his camera and snapped this picture," he explains.

A photograph released by the Japanese space agency, which had an agreement to buy images from Nasa, shows three luminous objects between the moon and the Apollo 13 craft. One is another cigar-shaped object which, we are told, is five miles long; the other two are more cylindrical, but are still huge, at about two miles in diameter.

Another slide–shot during Nasa's 1980 Voyager mission to Saturn–captures the "A" ring of the planet, with a cylindrical object sitting just outside the belt. Sgt Major Dean says the programme was launched to investigate "anomalous events" around Saturn. "The pictures they got back from Saturn were so stunning, so shocking that they simply locked them up in the safe."

The cylindrical object is self-luminous, "obviously man-made", and is larger than the moon. According to Sgt Major Dean, it was photographed moving in between the rings and around Saturn's moons.

Sgt Major Dean is the personification of gentleness and wisdom; the twang on his accent reminiscent of Jimmy Stewart. What would otherwise be amorphous blobs on the screen become symbols of technological transcendence. Accompanied by his emotive descriptions, there can be no denying their power. The audience responds warmly to his plea to end the "cover-up". Many rise to their feet.

"One of the shocking realities that we will be forced to face is that they are everywhere. We know of their certain presence in several permanent locations on the planet and we have photographic evidence of their presence in near space and throughout the solar system," says Sgt Major Dean.

We are left guessing for a while as to what his last image depicts. An aerial photograph of some kind of geometric structure, not unlike a complex of buildings or an airport. Not an airport, Sgt Major Dean says, "it's very likely a space port". "This facility is located on the equator [of Mars]. If you are interested in launching a vehicle from a planet, you put it on the equator and you take advantage of the rotation of the planet, the momentum, to assist in the launch."

In his book, *The Monuments of Mars*, Richard Hoagland asserted that the red planet was littered with ancient ruins. Although evidence of advanced life on other planets is difficult to verify beyond photographs, what about closer to home?

Klaus Dona may be short in stature but his voice needs no technological enhancement. The power of his oration is only matched by the mind-boggling photographs of artefacts and skeletons he has documented over 10 years while curator of the Habsburg Haus of Austria.

None of these artefacts should exist according to traditional science. In archaeological parlance they are "oo-parts".

A disc made from lydite found in Columbia depicts the process of fertilisation: male sperms, female egg cells and genitals; the fertilised egg; the foetus and the growing embryo each carved into sections of the stone. The other side shows what could be cell division and the developmental stages of frog-like creatures. The "genetic disc" does not fit within the known systems of South American cultures, but nonetheless suggests an astonishing knowledge of biological processes by an ancient society. Then there are the precision-engineered gynaecological instruments, also made of lydite, that fit perfectly into the hand and could not be replicated using today's technology, due to the hardness of the stone.

Many cultures have legends about giants, but here too Mr Dona presents evidence of their existence—numerous photographs of massively elongated skulls; bones from 7.6 metre tall humans in Ecuador and ancient cement footprints in South Africa that are 120cm long.

The "gold aircraft" found at the Tolima tombs in Columbia and dating from about 500AD have been tested in wind tunnels and air-worthy reconstructions made, suggesting that these could be models of ancient airplanes that once flew.

Mr Dona has analysed about 1,700 anomalous pieces, which are now mainly kept in secret private collections. They have to been seen to be believed.

Many of the attendees convene to a huge dining hall, where a buffet is on offer. I sit down beside a couple from Andorra, on the outskirts of Barcelona. Jonaina Perez is surprised that a British newspaper has taken the issue seriously enough to send over a reporter. After regaling me with descriptions of the Andorra countryside, she mentions matter-of-factly that she and her husband once saw a craft the size of the hall hover above them while out walking in the mountains. Her husband perhaps takes my open mouth to be a lack of understanding, and confirms the story in English. To them this is not science fiction, but a tangible reality. They, like many at this event, seek answers about a subject that their elected officials will rarely even acknowledge.

In the 1950s, a number of people began to come forward with claims of having had physical contact with human looking representatives of extraterrestrial civilisations. These "contactees" claimed to have been shown advanced technologies and been appraised of plans to assist humanity in becoming part of a galactic society where open contact with off-world civilisations would take place.

As the contactee stories began to disseminate into the wider populace, powerful figures in the security services of the US and other major nations began to take notice. The information provided by these people was perceived as a national security threat by some policy makers due to a technological gap–not least militarily–between these ETs and national governments.

The message of peacefully transforming the planet and ending the development of nuclear weapons drew support from thousands of people as the contactees travelled widely and spoke at conferences.

"Directly confronted were the policies of major nations that were actively building nuclear weapons. Thus contactees presented an urgent national security need for an extensive counter-intelligence programme," says Dr Salla. "Preventing the contactee movement from becoming a catalyst for global changes through the teachings and experiences gained from extraterrestrials became a top priority."

According to Dr Salla, the CIA played a key role in creating the necessary legal, political and social environment for the debunking of UFO reports and contactee claims. Reports of flying saucers were construed as a national security threat insofar as mass hysteria over them could be exploited by foreign enemies. Justification for this approach was found in the 1938 radio broadcast by Orson Welles of *War of the Worlds*, which had supposedly caused panic in some parts of America.

The Psychological Strategy Board was created following a presidential directive in 1951 to "authorise and provide for the more effective planning, co-ordination, and conduct within the framework of approved national policies, of psychological operations". The PSB was an interagency group that was initially located within the CIA but reported to the National Security Council. It's function was ostensibly to deal with the Cold War threat through psychological operations. However, Dr Salla says leaked documents show that the PSB was also concerned with the security threat posed by flying saucer reports and how they could undermine the authority of the US government.

Thus began an information war that many at the conference claim continues today.

Dr Salla cites The National Enquirer as a chief instrument in the psychological campaign against contactees and UFO reports, with its sensationalistic style discouraging "serious" reporters and researchers from investigating these stories.

"It succeeded so well that influential UFO researchers determined to establish the scientific merit of investigating UFO reports became unwitting allies to the covert psychological programme to dismiss contactee claims," he says.

There are those at the summit who claim to have regular contact with ETs.

Dr Steven Greer gave up a career as a Virginia emergency room doctor after founding The Disclosure Project. On May 9, 2001, Dr Greer presided over a press conference at the National Press Club in Washington, DC, where more than 20 military, government, intelligence and corporate witnesses presented testimonies regarding the existence of extraterrestrial life forms on the planet, and the reverse engineering of energy and propulsion systems from alien craft.

Dr Greer, whose uncle helped design the first lunar module, is also a director of the Center for the Study of Extraterrestrial Intelligence (CSETI). During his presentation, he shows footage of himself with a group of 50 people gathered at a car park in Pensacola, Florida. They signal into the night sky with a high-powered laser pointer. Amazingly, what were a group of white specks among the stars begin flashing back. Their monitoring equipment suddenly springs to life, with patterned beeps, not unlike Morse code signals. Dr Greer identifies the source of the signals as coming from the direction of the Orion constellation.

He says the Phoenix lights incident in 1999 was a close encounter of the fifth kind–orchestrated by his team ahead of a briefing with the president and members of the US Congress. Thousands of people reported seeing a triangular formation of lights pass over the state, which were broadcast live on Fox News. "When we asked the ETs for help, this is what showed up... a huge craft. It was a beautiful sight."

Dr Greer maintains that the speed of light is too slow for galactic communication. If ET wanted to phone home using BT or AT&T, then even for a call to a nearby star, say a thousand light years away, it would take 2,000 years–half that time to arrive and the other half to be returned.

"All inter-stellar technologies are trans-dimensional. And the heart of that science is consciousness, because they have technologies that interface directly with thought–coherent thought... We have discovered the Rosetta stone of extraterrestrial contact, and it's not the SETI project, it's not radio telescopes, it's not rockets, and it is not even pulsed microwaves. There are technologies that transcend directly into thought and awareness."

Dr Greer has developed protocols for ET contact that involve deep states of consciousness where, he says, it is possible to remote view the location of ET vehicles, and then contact them with a coherent stream of thought. They can then be "vectored" into a location, the same way a jet is directed into an airport. "They almost always come," he says.

"People need to understand that if it's inter-stellar, then it's going to be strange. If isn't strange, then it's probably a man-made device... Each of us carries within us the universal communicator, and it's called conscious awareness."

Dr Greer cites the work of Erwin Schrodinger, the Austrian physicist and the father of quantum mechanics, to support his assertions. Schrodinger said "the total number of minds in the universe in one; that is, it is a singularity. And so we see all these hundreds of people ... we all have our individualities, but shining through that unique window is the same light of consciousness. We divide it up and separate ourselves , but we can just as easily become still and peaceful, and become one again."

His group plans a mass-contact event in the Arizona desert in October.

In his efforts to bring about full disclosure about an ET presence on Earth, Dr Greer has briefed high ranking government, military and intelligence officials in the US and Europe–including, in 1993, CIA director R. James Woolsey and President Clinton. Most recently, his group has prepared a dossier for the Obama administration.

Stephen Bassett is hopeful that the "truth embargo" will be lifted under Barack Obama's presidency. Mr Basset, the founder of Paradigm Research Group, a Washington lobby group for disclosure, sees the current administration as one bookend of the truth embargo, with its opposite end being the alleged cover-up of the Roswell incident in New Mexico in 1947.

It seems the pressure to come clean is mounting, not least from the ET's themselves, as reported sightings and contact events are increasing. Hollywood has played it part, too, with some of the highest grossing movies of all time featuring extraterrestrials.

"Each year the polling data shows that public awareness of the ET issue grows; the number of people who think the government is lying grows. About 50 per cent believe the UFO phenomenon is ET in origin; about 20 per cent believe they have had a sighting; with about 10 per cent saying they have had direct contact with extraterrestrials," says Mr Bassett.

"Since the Cold War ended in 1991, the emergence of witnesses–people who have worked in government; people in authority, politicians, the military, members of civilian agencies–who have come forward has grown, and continues to grow."

Perhaps two of the most credible witnesses were the astronauts Col Gordon Cooper and Dr Edgar Mitchell. Col Cooper was one of America's first astronauts, taking part in Project Mercury in 1963, and Dr Mitchell was part of the Apollo 14 mission in 1971. Both men claimed to have seen strange things while in space and spent much of their retirement campaigning for disclosure of the US government's "X-files".

"I don't know what the ETs are going to do, but I know the public can do a lot and we are doing everything we can to get the public opinion to exert that pressure to end this truth embargo," says Mr Bassett.

He cites the lack of media coverage given to the Rockefeller Initiative, where Laurance Rockefeller, the billionaire philanthropist, approached Bill and Hillary Clinton in 1995 with "the best available evidence" on UFOs. Mr Bassett claims Mr Clinton eventually backed away from becoming "the disclosure president".

With many of the key players in that initiative–not least John Podesta and Bill Richardson–now associated with the Obama administration, Mr Bassett is confident that the floodgates will be opened in the US before long. And what is the ace in the hole of this release of information? "ET tech," as Mr Bassett calls it. In other words, access to methods of producing clean, free energy–as derived from the hitherto "secret" research into crashed UFOs and the like. Fibre optics, night-vision cameras and non-stick surfaces are just some of the alleged ET-derived "inventions".

Should the US authorities follow the lead of other nations and release its X-files, this may well precipitate something of a paradigm shift in consciousness for the planet–with the realisation that we are no longer an isolated civilisation floating in space, but part of a galactic society. And then when and where, and how, would first contact take place?

Paola Harris has spent much of her career charting witness testimonies and collecting photographic evidence of the ET phenomenon. Ms Harris, whose father was an Italian diplomat to the US, has developed, what she calls, protocols for contact.

The issue of how to interact with other cosmic civilisations has been considered in the past. Albert Einstein and Robert Oppenheimer, who both worked on the atomic bomb project and who had noticed an increase in UFO activity at the White Sands site in New Mexico, drafted a document in the 1940s asking who on the planet would speak for us and what could we learn from these outsiders. The document, directed at President Truman, mooted the idea of a "supra-United Nations", which would be empowered to deal with the emerging issue of exopolitics.

"When a contact happens, who do they go to–the country with the most people? The country with the most power at that time?" says Ms Harris. "We need some kind of international forum on this."

Last year the Vatican had a disclosure of its own in L'Osservatore Romano, its official newspaper.

"Father [Gabriel] Funes, who is the new head of the Vatican observatory, said three things: number one; it is not against your religion to believe in UFO's; number two; they are our brothers and sisters; and number three–and this is the one that blew me away–he said, Jesus did not need to die for the extraterrestrials because they were not born with original sin. Why did he say this? Is he getting ready for a new world view that's coming, because he knows something is going to happen?" she asks.

The Vatican seems to be saying that Jesus did not have to go to all the other planets to die.

To some of these delegates, Nasa stands for "never a straight answer". With the burden of evidence growing and the disclosure movement spreading around the world, perhaps we can expect some straighter answers in the near future?

If extraterrestrials have been visiting us since well into antiquity, occasionally leaving a trace in the sky or in a farmer's field, where is the mass invasion mooted by our science fiction writers and military commanders? Maybe they are just playing a waiting game? Waiting for us to put aside our paranoia and parochial views–until such time as we gaze out at the stars and recognise that we are part of a galactic society.

Some Minor Revisions

By James Zul

A howling Siberian wind rattled the large bay window, like a frozen hand reaching out from a far-flung gulag, beckoning him to that purgatory for dissidents, thought Dmitri Shostakovich. Though, judging by the inch of ice on the inside of the window, it might even be colder inside than out, he concluded.

His best compositions arrived when he was hopeful, or at least determined. What flow of creativity could come from a catatonic mind and body; the former paralysed by the fear, the latter incapacitated by cold. Action! Yes, he thought, a way to deal with both. Shostakovich reached out to a copy of Pravda sitting on the table. Dated June 28, 1936, it had been in his possession for six months, since he lifted it from a kiosk on the main street in Arkhangelsk one sunny morning. The demonic effect of its lead editorial–entitled "Muddle Instead of Music," undoubtedly penned by Stalin himself–had only grown in power over that period.

Scrunching the paper in his hand, Shostakovich shuffled over to the barren mantle and struck a match under it. The flames illuminated the room–and rekindled the memory of that brilliant sunny day. The clouds had not been long coming after the attack on his beloved opera, Lady Macbeth of Mtsensk. In one fell swoop, he had been transformed from national hero to pariah of the state.

That day, he had halted outside the town hall; the otherwise blackened façade emblazoned with the city's coat of arms–a blue and red angel surmounting a silhouetted devil. How he had prayed for such an intervention, to banish the nascent evils in his life.

But now, once again, the grey hue of the room returned, as the flickering ashes of the fireplace reclaimed their momentary golden halo.

Shostakovich slumped back into his chair. The pages of musical notations sprawled across his desk seemed like a death warrant instigated and authorised by his own hand. What of the hidden motifs and themes of dissent underpinning this and his other symphonies? The Great Leader would interpret them as obsequious formalities, but perhaps if he had the intelligence to discern, or was told, their real counter-cultural significance, he, 35-year-old Shostakovich, might gain a new-found respect in his eyes?

"Zatknis!"–he swiped the manuscripts onto the floor–more mind games, more self-betrayal. Look at him–a quivering wreck, just like Prokofiev. Any resistance beyond subliminal cues could only lead to death, or worse… Look at the fate of his mother-in-law, Sofiya Varzar, an astronomer–sent to the camp in Karaganda;

his patron, Marshal Tukhachevsky–shot shortly after his arrest; Boris Kornilov and Adrian Piotrovsky–dear friends who disappeared during the night. Not a chance to grieve before it happened again. When will be the knock on *his* door? Irina, his dear wife, had spent the past month sleeping alone; he had not yet managed to convince her that his bedding down in the hallway was out of genuine consideration. When the secret police did come for him, he would at least spare her the indignity of being seen in a nightgown.

Only thirteen hours to go before the performance; too late for them to cancel now; he would carry this symphony into the last chance saloon, as the Bolshoi must now be considered by all Soviet composers–the bittersweet sip of nectar as the barrel runs dry.

Shostakovich lifted a cigarette to his mouth; the orange explosion of sulphur momentarily found expression on his spectacles' bulbous lenses. He dragged hard, but the primordial relief from the glowing embers was soon quenched by the cold logic of his physician; a mantra now embedded in his subconscious: "Everything rests on the breath; but the breath rests on the lungs." Another dictator, thought Shostakovich.

A deep sigh petered out as a groan. Tics and grimaces spontaneously erupted across his face, and then subsided, as the timid, brilliant personality surrendered all to despair. The cigarette dropped onto the varnished floor as he drifted off into oblivion.

A gust from the chimney flamed the hearth. Sparks floated out towards the slumped figure. The eyes darted from side to side beneath their veils. A subtle change registered on the face; now at peace; the pursed lips inverted, almost smiling. Daylight gradually retreated from the room; but his angular features remained bathed in an orange glow, held in place amid the black void.

The stillness was suddenly shattered by a rat, tat, tat on the door. Its hinges creaked defiantly. The gaunt but ferocious-looking housekeeper marched into the room. "Dmitri Dmitryevich Shostakovich, time to get up. This is the big day," said Natalya Sobranie Mikhailovna, her husky voice an indictment of the eponymous cigarette brand. She stood over him. An eyelid twitched. He held up his hands to block out the brilliant white of her starched blouse. The reality of his night odyssey returned—something still etched on the back of his eyelids; a concept that must be grasped and held in the mind. Shostakovich rose to his feet, and ushered her towards the door. He dropped the latch and stumbled over to his desk. Paper, paper, he must find paper!

Grasping for a pen, he scribbled frantically, trying to hold out the din of the waking mind. Nothing must halt the flow of wisdom, the majesty of the idea must be given form. One sheet after another filled with notation: cleffs consorting with quarter tones; alla breve followed by glissando; crescendo begetting stacatto. Finally, he held the pile of notes aloft, transparent under the streaming sunlight.

Again, rat, tat, tat on the door. "Dmitri, Isaak Berlinsky is here," bellowed Natalya.

"Show him in," muttered Shostakovich.

A fair-haired stick of a man glided in through the open door. His face was pained.

"Dmitri, our rehearsal, have you forgotten?" exclaimed Isaak.

Shostakovich handed him the new notations. "Part II, allegro. This is to replace it."

"Are you..." Shostakovich cut him short with an out-stretched hand.

"They are minor revisions. Get the orchestra ready."

Isaak turned on his feet, then glanced back. "I was expecting the Order of Lenin for this performance. Now, at the last moment, you decide to play games."

Shostakovich mused to himself on their differing expectations. "Isaak, you are blessed with a kind of naivety. You expect the best outcome for yourself, and you invariably get it. I have much to learn from you."

Isaak shook his head in disapproval and padded away. Shostakovich stood in the sun-drenched room, now brimming with possibility–what seemed an insurmountable dilemma last night was now a call to adventure.

Somewhere in the city a bell tolled. The grand, pillared entrance to the Bolshoi theatre filtered the shoal of incoming bourgeoisie. The uniform of dinner jackets and gowns was never enough to support the pretence at proletariat égalité; the aristocrats were betrayed by their prominent noses and the social climbers by their self-conscious waddle. Nevertheless, inside the auditorium, all were peasants under the gaze of the feudal lord.

Silence descended on the hall. A curtain twitched at the back of the "Tsar's" box. A nervous-looking attendant gave a final cursory inspection of the seats and refreshments. The curtain parted and the ridged, leather face of Stalin emerged from the shadows. He was followed by Party Secretary Andrei Zhdanov–whose crinkled features offset the smooth lines of his quasi-naval uniform.

A huge crystal chandelier hovered below the arched ceiling, competing for attention with extravagant gold reliefs and murals.

Shostakovich scuttled along a trench below the stage and took a seat in the murky pit facing the orchestra. He craned up to take in a view of the box. Stalin and Zhdanov sat against scarlet draping. No other colour would be appropriate, thought Shostakovich–blood does not run any other hue.

There was a clang of instruments as a troop of male choristers filed on stage and squeezed in behind the brass section. The lead violinist–a hairy Ukrainian in his mid-50s–glared quizzically at Shostakovich, who returned an authoritative wave. The sprightly Isaak made his way to the podium. He bowed to the audience and then to the box. He tapped his baton on the wooden stand. Silence. On his mark, the first movement began. Its brooding tone evoked the cold temperatures outside; violas and cellos maintained the sense of inertia–its elusions to the rigid political regime would be obvious to all but the most cretinous listeners. As bassoons, trombones and piano unfolded the audience was taken on a journey that undulated and mellowed, reaching a climactic fanfare of trumpets.

Isaak lapped up the applause. He squinted down at Shostakovich, whose glasses glinted back; the invisible bond of trust between composer and conductor held firm.

The obligatory coughs and splutters died out. The air was once again static. A few faces in the crowd turned in the direction of their leader; whose profile probably adorned a wall in their homes—safely restrained behind glass and wooden frame. In the flesh, however, it was so grisly and three-dimensional that even a momentary glance brought the risk of a peptic ulcer.

The conductor took a deep breath; his arms gradually levitated; then struck downward with lightening speed; a ten-drum blast seared the air. Stalin jumped in his seat. Gasps from the audience invaded the momentary void. The conductor flinched again and the drums rumbled back to life; this time low and deep, in deference to the preceding explosion. The rum, bum, bum grew in intensity. The Muscovites sat prone as if expecting a siege; all eyes fixed on the penguin-suited man out front. What magic was he conjuring, they wondered? Surely nothing to challenge the ferocious beast in their midst?

The steady rumble of wood on bear skin was supplemented by the haunting echo of the choral troop. Stalin tapped his finger on the balcony... his head nodded gently, unable to resist the primal rhythm. Animal motifs and human demigods danced together in the invisible ether. The sharpness of the gilded frescoes and glistening instruments began to blur as the octave universe asserted its all-encompassing vibration, materialising in a kaleidoscope of chromaticism.

Irritation registered on the leader's face. He edged his seat back, as if to stand, but then stiffened: the mind commanded but the body defied. Some deep cellular memory empathised with the real master of ceremony; a phantom of the aural world now manifest and malignant.

Would his arm only obey, he would summon a guard and have the maestro below executed on the spot. Anything to make it stop.

Faces turned towards the Tsar's box. Stalin sat immobile, catatonic. The unfolding dance of sound was not yet done. Shockwaves streamed out on every prompt of the baton. Only the tyrant's eyes betrayed the internal confusion; an agony not borne with the fortitude of a gulag inmate, but nonetheless imposed by some immutable force. Violas, violins and cellos united in a sea of swirling screeches, before washing out over the stage; the conductor left to paw the air helplessly.

Stalin slavishly followed the movement of a shadowy mist; his dilated pupils stretched to breaking point. The auditorium was now only a dream; the will of harmonics held sway.

Shostakovich sat in a deep trance; his body freed of its habitual tension; the thin mouth plumped and parted.

The door to his subconscious was unlocked once more. But what had been released that now twisted and writhed in mid air; drawn towards a human target? Terror had taken form; a foretaste of horrors to come under a maniacal personality–the etheric preceding the material.

The hanging ball of crystal began to grow in lustre; a low hum summoned Stalin's attention. His unflinching stare enveloped the million-watt orb; a light that now revealed infinite potential; a miniature cosmos, no less. The radiating energy embraced him, understood him; celebrated him. A unifying force; something not yet conceived in his inadequate existence. Understanding seeped into the gross matter of his mind; light, vibration and hum revealed as the underlying fabric of reality. All was equal and yet individuated under this overarching triumvirate. His cruelty and malice now melted like butter.

Shostakovich woke with a start. Isaak pulled at his arm. "Wake up. They are shutting the doors."

Shostakovich looked around at the empty hall. "I was dreaming. Have I slept through everything?"

"It would seem so," countered Isaak. "Come now and I will drop you off."

Shostakovich dismounted from the carriage outside his home. He turned to Isaak. "How did he take it tonight?"

"There were no obvious eruptions from the box. People wondered if he had taken ill. Let us leave it at that … until the morning. As you know, I am ever the optimist."

The first light of day and the loud snap of the letterbox conspired to raise Shostakovich from his slumber. He looked over at his wife, who remained buried in her pillow. He pattered over to the bedroom door and peeked out at the hall. A tightly rolled copy of Pravda sat propped against the door. He snatched it up and pulled off the binding. As he scanned the front page, his mouth dropped open. He read again the splash headlines: "Stalin Joins Monastic Order... Leader Renounces Belief in Lenin...Politicians Scramble to Form Senate." Shostakovich took a deep breath and scratched his head.